PENGUIN

ARKANA

WOMEN IN SEARCH OF THE SACRED

Anne Bancroft spent the early part of her life in the Quaker village of Jordans. While her four children were growing up she became a lecturer in comparative religion and at the same time began her own quest for spiritual understanding. Over the years she has found strength and inspiration in Buddhism and a deepening understanding of western mysticism. She is the author of several other books on religion and mysticism, including *Origins of the Sacred* (Arkana, 1987), *Weavers of Wisdom: Women Mystics of the Twentieth Century* (Arkana, 1989) and *Twentieth Century Mystics and Sages* (Arkana, 1989).

D0279905

Anne Bancroft

—

WOMEN IN SEARCH
OF THE SACRED

ARKANA
PENGUIN BOOKS

ARKANA

Published by the Penguin Group
Penguin Books Ltd, 27 Wrights Lane, London w8 5tz, England
Penguin Books USA Inc., 375 Hudson Street, New York, New York 10014, USA
Penguin Books Australia Ltd, Ringwood, Victoria, Australia
Penguin Books Canada Ltd, 10 Alcorn Avenue, Toronto, Ontario, Canada m4v 3b2
Penguin Books (NZ) Ltd, 182–190 Wairau Road, Auckland 10, New Zealand

Penguin Books Ltd, Registered Offices: Harmondsworth, Middlesex, England

First published 1996
1 3 5 7 9 10 8 6 4 2

Typeset in 10/12pt Monotype Baskerville
by Datix International Limited, Bungay, Suffolk
Printed in England by Clays Ltd, St Ives plc

Contents

Acknowledgements

With many thanks to Debbie and Eddie Shapiro, my daughter and son-in-law, who are also writers in this field, for their excellent suggestions.

The author and publishers also gratefully acknowledge permission to use extracts from the following copyright works: *The Green Knight* by Iris Murdoch. Copyright © 1993 by Iris Murdoch. To Penguin Books Canada Ltd, Random House UK Ltd and Viking Penguin, a division of Penguin Books USA Inc.; *Metaphysics as a Guide to Morals* by Iris Murdoch. Copyright © 1992 by Iris Murdoch. To Chatto & Windus and Viking Penguin, a division of Penguin Books USA Inc.; *The Nice and the Good* by Iris Murdoch. Copyright © 1968 by Iris Murdoch. To Random House UK Ltd and Viking Penguin, a division of Penguin Books USA Inc.; *The Sovereignty of Good* by Iris Murdoch (Routledge, 1991). To International Thomson Publishing Services Ltd; *Pilgrim at Tinker's Creek* and *Teaching a Stone to Talk* by Annie Dillard. To the author and Blanche C. Gregory, Inc.

Introduction

A special sense of the holiness and seriousness of existence is shared by all the participants in this book. They have a passion for the sacred and have directed their lives to the perception of its wonder. For each of them it manifests in a different way and each chapter shows a distinct and unique path. The treading of that path in the midst of a life which was sometimes in turmoil – three of the women were caught up in revolutions – is the substance of the book. Such a committed journey is also the spiritual challenge of our time and one to which each of us can respond.

For the nun Elaine MacInnes, for instance, who went as a missionary to Japan and became a Zen teacher, the sacred is revealed in the silence of Zen meditation; while for the philosopher and novelist Iris Murdoch, it is to be found in the Good. For Susan Howatch, the author of six bestselling novels on the psychology of religion in the Church of England, it is discovered through alignment to God's will. Danah Zohar, a physicist and a philosopher, sees it in the wonder of life as revealed by quantum physics. Marianne Williamson, a non-denominational minister, a Hollywood guru and a thinker and spiritual writer, finds it by way of surrender to the Holy Spirit; while for Annie Dillard, winner of the Pulitzer Prize and a botanist and mystic, it continues to reveal itself in the intricate marvels of the natural world. It is manifested by way of the Pagan gods dwelling within the archetypes of the mind for Vivianne Crowley, a High Priestess of Wicca. Ma Yoga Shakti, born in India, and with ashrams in America and India, follows it by way of the path of yoga. Jung Chang, the Chinese author and one-time Red Guard and devotee of Mao, discovered it in the integrity and balance of her own and others' lives during persecution. And it is present for Sheila Cassidy, a doctor tortured and imprisoned in Chile, in all who suffer.

Many men could equally well have appeared in these pages, but this book is about women. We are witnessing, after a very long time, the arising of feminine values – in both men and women – as women transform their lives and learn to live in mature dignity and freedom. The earlier masculine 'rational' thinking that brought about the separation of the self from nature is giving way to a reuniting of the self with the ground of its being and a healing of the person with the planet and with every form of life. A book such as this – indeed, this particular one – celebrates the acknowledgement that the feminine is at last beginning to balance the masculine and that after many centuries women are moving out of the invisibility of hidden service and into the open commitment of a life in the world lived with a spiritual purpose – the search for the sacred.

Transformation lies at the very heart of life and is the key to all that we are. Without growth and transformation we remain bound in a web of ignorance and delusion. The desire to be transformed, to grow into new perception and new freedom is the call which the women in this book have clearly heard and to which each has responded in her own way. There are many of us throughout the world who feel as they do and who are learning to shed the burden of worn-out beliefs and concepts, and to embrace the evolution of the spirit as it discovers and rejoices in the sacred.

It is a journey which has magnetic power and draws us continually onwards. When the spiritual dimension breaks in upon the everyday world of thought and feeling, we know the journey has begun. Our conventional life may be broken wide open, because to discover the sacred is to change our priorities. Every object and every event may acquire a new significance as the actual life of oneself, in its homely detail, becomes lived in the light of eternity. Personal existence assumes meaning and direction. Pervading us is a sense of deep and steady security which knowledge of the ultimate alone can bring. It may seem that one has at last emerged from childhood into maturity.

It is from this security that we can, both women and men, learn to give ourselves completely to the world we live in, caring for it and bonding with it so that we are connected at every point to the sacred. For the sacred is no other than where we are at this moment. If we do not feel that, then our perception must change, and throughout the world there is a change now taking place. Breaking through the old concept of two separate dimensions, the everyday and the spiritual, is a new understanding that they are one and that this relative and mortal world in which we live is no other than the absolute and infinite world of the sacred itself.

The women who feature in this book are those who can articulate for us some of the journey, some of the discoveries and some of the wisdom and understanding that comes from the breakthrough, from knowing that transformation is in this moment where we are now. The rest is for us to discover in ourselves as we learn to reunite and reconnect with the sacred ground of our being.

Elaine MacInnes

'Zen is a discipline that leads eventually to a direct experience of Nothingness and union. This experience then seeks to express itself in compassion.'

Of all the religious disciplines Zen Buddhism is perhaps the least esoteric, the most bare and the most simple. In fact it is so bare that many people do not regard it as the branch of a religion at all, including many Zen masters and Sister Elaine MacInnes. Yet it has had such a powerful influence on her life that we should look at what it is and how she, a Roman Catholic nun, came across it.

So, first, what is Zen? It is a contemplative practice, says Sister Elaine, and a way of liberation. As such it goes beyond all religions: 'Zen has no concepts and it is neither religious nor philosophical. Rather, it points directly to the heart–mind. When practised, this pointing ripens into experience in a way which is transforming, helping the person awaken to his or her essential nature.'

And what is the practice? Essentially it is silence. It is an inner silence in which one can 'listen to the teacher and one's own body and mind and to the universe itself and all the ten thousand things'.

Beginners today, she tells us, are cautioned to:

1. Allow themselves to be emptied.
2. Let go, so they will have no fear of emptiness.
3. Give up their busyness, which most often has nothing to do with professional duties.

Psychologists warn us, she says, that in today's world 'we often exhaust our mind in egotistical pursuits, a mind already alienated by an illusory fear of separation. The antidote is living life in awareness and then eventually coming to "see" that the world is One and we are in that Oneness. There is no separation at all, and things are just as they are.

'Silence is the shaft we descend to the depths of contemplation. Silence is the vehicle that takes us to the innermost centre of our being which is the place for all authentic practice.

'Lao Tzu tells us that silence is the great revelation. What does it tell us? Well, many things along the way in daily transformation but eventually it reveals the Self. When we come to know this True Self, we come to know who we are.'

But before we travel further into the silence of Zen let us find out how Sister Elaine arrived at the understanding which illuminates her life. She was born, she tells us, in Canada on the east coast, to a loving Catholic family. Her mother was a musician and the whole family played music together – Elaine, the violin. She went to a convent and remembers her childhood as happy but uneventful. God was taken for granted but not particularly thought about.

When she left school she went on to the famous Juilliard school of music in New York and there she was asked a question that struck her as strange. She was standing outside her practice studio one day when an unknown young man came up, took her by the shoulders and said, with great urgency, 'There *is* a God, isn't there? There has to be.' She was so surprised, she said the first thing that came into her head: 'If I were you, I wouldn't worry. I think you'll find that there is, and that everything's OK.' He went away but the question left her also with a sense of urgency, as though it were something that she too had to find out.

But life went on. It was wartime and ten thousand British soldiers were being sent to New Brunswick, to her very home town, to train. Elaine and one of the soldiers fell in love and she visualized a life in England. But later in the war he was killed, and this was a hard blow.

The young man's question still returned from time to time to haunt her but nevertheless it was not for some years that its urgency came back and it was then that she felt a call to become a nun. She joined Our Lady's Missionaries, a Canadian foreign mission community, for reasons, she confesses, that were largely romantic: she had a vision of South Sea Islands and eager brown people round a fire at night time. But the reality of life as a nun was very different and she found it extremely hard after her years of loving life and living it to the full to submit to what often seemed petty discipline. She was twenty-nine. But, as she says, she was not a quitter and was determined to stick it out for a bit at least, feeling it would be indecent to leave too soon. And then, suddenly, her feeling for God catapulted. She came across a small book, *One with Jesus* by a Jesuit called Diega. In spite of finding the title off-putting, she opened the book and for the first time read about the indwelling of the divine spirit. This was to nourish her for six years and she found herself connected to the sacred within the world as well as within herself. She felt, for the first time, that she was really being true to herself.

She found she loved meditation. It was obligatory at the convent to write out meditations based on a phrase in the Bible. In the evening the novices were given the phrase and then in the morning, as soon as they got up and when the Office had been chanted, they started the meditation. Elaine would write all her thoughts, what she heard and what she saw, and to begin with it was very flamboyant. But after a time she got tired of writing in this way and it became simpler.

Then Elaine decided she needed more help and the novice mistress, even in a small town in Ontario, managed to buy some fifty books, big tomes of prayer and instruction. Elaine read them all and found they meant nothing to her. Her little book *One with Jesus* still sustained her and she developed a strong relationship to the 'indwelling God'.

Within the convent the nuns read the lives of the saints together and Elaine could never stand the over-pious accounts. But one book on St Francis Xavier, a remarkable sixteenth-century Jesuit missionary, who spent many years in Japan and whose practical mysticism and kindness of manner founded Christianity there, did interest her deeply. Elaine, who had begun to experience a great desire to go to Japan, set up a secret deal with Xavier: if you'll get me to Japan, I'll get up Mount Hiei and be received by a monk (Xavier had made an attempt at Mount Hiei but had never managed to get to the top to meet the renowned monk who lived in the temple there). Quite soon she was sent to Japan.

She did not go as a simple missionary, however, as she had far too much respect for the culture she was entering. As she was a trained concert violinist, and since the Japanese liked classical western music, she decided that her best possible path as a missioner would be to share what she could of her talent in return for learning about Buddhism and Japanese religion. At the start of her journey to Japan she met a young theologian who reinforced this view by saying: 'I hope you're not going to Japan for any other reason but to learn.' When she arrived she saw how realistic this advice was. 'I soon discovered that the Japanese had an extremely ancient culture of their own. And not only did it express their deepest feelings, but also it entered almost every facet of their culture and daily life.'

First she went for two years to a language school to learn Japanese. It was while she was there that she decided she had better fulfil her side of the bargain to climb Mount Hiei. A friend at the language school, who had been up to the temple at the top several times, said she would take her. When they reached the temple they were met by a remarkable Zen monk who was completing a twelve-year period of solitary living. He prepared tea for them in silence. Finally he coughed and told Elaine's friend that she could introduce Elaine. After the introduction, his first question to her was, 'How do you pray?' She was nonplussed. 'What do you mean?' she asked.

'Well, for instance, your body position, how is it?'

'It doesn't make much difference,' Elaine replied.

'Oh, yes, it does!' he said. 'It makes a lot of difference!'

Then he proceeded to tell her about Zen and the way people sit in meditation. She and her friend listened enthralled until he held up his hand and said, 'Excuse me, but if you want to get back to Kyoto tonight, the last funicular is going down in about ten minutes.'

They began to rush away but suddenly Elaine stopped. 'I forgot what I came up here for! I came up to tell you about Francis Xavier.'

'Oh, I know all about him,' the monk said. 'He never reached the top,' and they both burst out laughing.

'I came up here to be received by you,' Elaine said.

'Well,' he replied, 'you can tell him in your prayer that you were very gratefully received.'

It was soon after that encounter that Elaine met one of the best known of modern Jesuit missionaries in Japan, Father Hugo Enomiya Lassalle, whom she told of her desire to learn about Zen. It was a time of great change within the Catholic Church and Pope John XXIII was bringing together bishops from around the world to persuade them to hold in respect all great religions for each contained truths which Catholics should search out if they were to know the full grandeur of the Infinite. Father Lassalle thus had no hesitation in helping her but he would not, however, let her study with him. 'You're learning Japanese and you're going to be here the rest of your life. You must go to the horse's mouth.' He intended that she should study with a master but Elaine had already made friends with some nuns and preferred to go to a convent, so he arranged that she went to Enkoji in Kyoto, a Zen convent which was in the hands of an abbess, Fukogai.

At the first interview Fukogai took one look at Elaine and said, 'You won't last ten minutes.' Elaine, who is made of tough material, replied, 'Well, start me off on five.' She stayed for eight years, but it was not an altogether happy time as Fukogai never relented in her attitude.

During Elaine's first days she was expected to attend sesshin, a period of intense meditation, sitting in the lotus position, when participants get up at three in the morning and have a fifteen-hour daily schedule, including four hours of manual work. 'I found it so hectic,' says Elaine, 'that I didn't get my face washed for three days.' It was bitterly cold for there was no heating although it was December. She had another interview with Fukogai who quoted the first sentence of the Lord's Prayer – 'Our Father Who art in heaven' – in some scorn. 'Ridiculous! How do you think you're going to get anywhere in Zen if you think your God is up in heaven?' Then she rang the bell for dismissal and Elaine had to leave. This was her initial experience of the famous interview technique – dokusan – in which the teacher is meant to test the pupil's understanding and give advice. Unlike Fukogai's use of sarcastic comment, it is usually conducted with understanding and compassion.

'It was a tough pull,' Elaine says. 'But I have a lot of determination and I learnt to sit and I sat and I sat. And then nice things began to happen to me. I could feel myself becoming lighter and lighter and it was *wonderful*.'

Every day during sesshin the nuns walked to another temple near by where a famous Zen master Shibayama gave teisho, talks on Zen. 'I never felt at home in the harshness of Enkoji,' says Elaine, 'but the thrusts in Shibayama's fine teisho were the catalysts I needed and account for the long period of time I spent in Enkoji.'

There is an ironic twist to the story of Fukogai and her unrelenting hostility to the Catholic Elaine. Many years later, and after some time away from Japan, Elaine returned for a visit. She was told that Fukogai had died. Fukogai's nuns had dispersed, but one of them, a friend of Elaine's, promised to take her to Fukogai's grave and when they met she presented Elaine with a package. Fukogai's possessions had gone to her blood sister, including the curved stick which was her badge of office and her most prized possession. It should have been cremated with her but by some oversight it was not, and her former nuns had all agreed that Elaine, the only one who was actually teaching Zen, should have it. So in the end, Fukogai's most precious treasure, her symbol of authority, went to the one woman she could never accept, the western nun.

After her eight years at Enkoji, Elaine was asked by Father Lassalle to help him run the first sesshin at a new Zen centre he had opened west of Tokyo. While the sesshin was in progress Elaine experienced a very strong makyo, an unusual psychic event. She tells us that being the overseer meant that she had much time to sit in meditation. Within a couple of days, she began to hear a radio. When she complained to the janitor, he told her there wasn't one in the area. The following day she noticed that the radio played only when she was sitting in meditation and was not busy in the kitchen or answering the phone.

'One afternoon while meditating, I was drowsy in the heat, and my head must have nodded. In any case, one of the rookie monitors rushed up, and without any indication of his intention, gave me a couple of good solid whacks with the kyosaku [a flat piece of wood administered between the shoulder blades, both to wake up the person and to ease spinal tension]. Immediately the "radio" burst into loud, majestic musical chords, which seemed to come from a heavenly organ. Its sound seemed to fill the entire universe, and lasted for several minutes. Then it gradually grew less in volume and within an hour or so disappeared completely. I never heard it again.'

She told Father Lassalle who arranged for her to attend the monastery of Yamada Koun Roshi. (Although the title Roshi merely means mature teacher, it is very highly regarded in Japan.) Yamada accepted Elaine at once. For some time he had been sympathetic to other religions and many Christians went to learn Zen from him. He had nuns, priests and seminarians among his disciples, to whom he brought new appreciation of their Christian faith. He did not want it to be otherwise. 'He did wonder why so many Christians came to him for guidance in prayer, and urged those of us whom he allowed to teach to give the Church a "shot in the arm" as far as contemplative prayer is concerned. But he had the highest regard for the Church. He was convinced that the lamp of illumination, the transmission of the true experience of enlightenment ... could be absorbed by all the world's great religions. "How you articulate that experience within the framework of your own religion is your responsibility," he used to tell us.'

While she was with Yamada Roshi, Elaine experienced kensho, a true enlightenment experience. ' "Ken" means to see and "sho" is your nature. So the experience means seeing your deepest nature, your deepest self. But it's the "see" that's the key to it. Sometimes we see things when they're just an inch away, sometimes a yard away, sometimes, if we have better sight, at six yards or a hundred yards. The substance is always the same but the clarity of your vision is much different. So there are small kenshos and there are deeper ones and deeper, and then there are really full ones.'

This experience is the first aim of the Zen training. There are many descriptions of it in Zen literature. The sixteenth-century Zen master Han-Shan says, 'I took a walk. Suddenly I stood still, filled with the realization that I had no body or mind. All I could see was one great illuminating Whole – perfect, lucid and serene. It was like an all-embracing mirror from which the mountains and the rivers of the earth were projected ... I felt clear and transparent.' And the thirteenth-century Dogen, in an ecstasy of release, shouted, 'Mind and body dropped off! Dropped off! Dropped off! This state must be experienced by you all. It is like piling fruit into a basket without a bottom, like pouring water into a bowl with a hole in it.' Hakuin, in the eighteenth century, said, 'All of a sudden you find your mind and body wiped out of existence. This is what is known as letting go your hold. As you regain your breath it is like drinking water and knowing it is cold. It is joy inexpressible.'

Elaine had the experience of everything dropping away, the fruit basket without a bottom to it, and afterwards felt everything had changed. The Nothingness transformed her and when she saw the world in relation to that Nothingness, she felt 'the most firm oneness with everything you could ever experience'. It took her back to a time in her childhood when she and her sisters were ill and her mother came into the room with two thermometers on a tray. Elaine managed to break both of them and started to play with the two pieces of mercury. To her great interest, they jumped together. Years later, when she experienced kensho, she felt the same sensation of the Nothingness and the universe suddenly 'going wham together! And it was absolutely *now*.' Looking back, she says, 'Before the oneness there really has to be an emptiness.' Yamada Roshi formally recognized her kensho. After she had been with him some time, he gave her his transmission and went through the procedure of making her a teacher.

This had all taken a number of years, in which Elaine had also organized a culture centre in Kyoto where she and others played music, and both eastern and western culture were explored. She was fully at home in Japan and became a great friend of Yamada Roshi and his wife.

We should take stock here of what she had really learnt to do. First there was the sitting. It is believed in Zen that sitting in the lotus posture – each leg folded into the other and spine straight – is the perfect position for the balance of mind and body and for allowing the breath to move in and out of the lungs freely. Oriental people manage it a great deal better than westerners and for westerners there is usually a good deal of discomfort until they get used to it. However, more merciful variations are also allowed. One is to kneel on a flat cushion called a zafu, and use a low stool or a small stuffed cushion to rest one's bottom on. Another (if one is *really* hopeless) is to sit on a chair with spine straight and feet flat on the ground. Whichever way one uses, the aim is 'to silence and harmonize the body and mind and breath, and in so doing come to a knowledge of our true selves'.

'How do we practise the Way of silence?' asks Elaine. 'The core of Zen practice is zazen, or sitting meditation. Zazen is often translated as contemplation, a kind of meditation that goes beyond the intellect, feeling, memory and imagination to a deeper level of consciousness.' Entering the silence of meditation is not easy however because thoughts come wandering in from all directions and distract the mind. So there has to be the growth of a 'mind position' as well as a body one.

'Just about all who come to us know that in Zen one stops the thinking process, but there is no real comprehension of what that entails. The nearest Christian word is contemplation and although

8

that word does not yet enjoy a very specific connotation, it is usually helpful at this stage to point out that John of the Cross defines contemplation as "cessation of sense and spiritual faculties". Not only do we disengage from linear thinking and even entertaining random thoughts, but also all feelings and rememberings and imaginings and planning, etc. In other words we disengage the psyche from all its busyness. For people living in the hub of today's world, this is a shift of gargantuan magnitude.'

When people first begin to sit in zazen they are taught an exercise to bring the mind to tranquillity. It is a very simple one – to count the breath.

'When sitting on the zafu, begin by inhaling and exhaling deeply three times. The exhalation should take twice as long as the inhalation. This is a good habit to form immediately, because it cuts off what went before, and also sets up the basis of a good breathing rhythm.

'Next watch your breath come in and out, in and out for a few sequences, and then start counting the breaths from one to ten. The inhalations will be the odd numbers and the exhalations the even. Breathe the way that is natural for you and count only to ten, and then repeat.

'Counting the breaths may sound easy, but in practice it is quite difficult to just count the breaths, without being distracted from the count by stray thoughts, memories, fantasies, etc. When you catch yourself being distracted from counting, or are losing the count altogether, simply resume counting from one.

'We gradually gain a little control of our superactive mind through this very simple expediency of breath-counting. It is not difficult but neither is it easy to maintain for a sizable period of time. One roshi friend said he had a beginner who never got past number one in his counting!

'On our cushion, we do the practice of breath-counting. Away from the cushion, we are aware of being. By that is meant that we are where we are and we do what we are doing. For instance, if we are washing the dishes, our body and mind are absorbed in harmony while performing that task. We so often fall into separation by allowing our mind to wander where it will, such as thinking of other things while washing dishes.

'Separation is the arch-enemy of all life. Indeed the word "diabolical" is from the Greek word *diaballein*, to separate or divide. So separation is the work of the devil, and let us away with it. In all our waking moments, let us try to be where our body is, and not separated from the work or play in which we are engaged. When we complete one task, we drop it cleanly and proceed to the next encounter, in awareness.'

Almost all Zen practice revolves around such attention to the present moment. True awareness of the moment brings about the remarkable feeling that there is no limit to its wonder. Here and now is 'itself' and 'itself' is something so profound that we can only gasp in awe. So attention to the immediate now is the way of Zen carried out in daily life. But like all simple-sounding practices it is not always easy or obvious and indeed it is often underrated. There is a Zen story that a roshi was asked by respectful monks what was the secret of enlightenment. 'Attention,' he replied, giving them just the one word. They were baffled. Surely this was not all. 'Could you tell us more?' they begged. 'Certainly,' he answered. 'Attention, attention.'

In daily life, then, attention is brought to bear fully on what we are doing so that each action is lived in the present. In the zendo, this discipline is applied to sitting on the cushion and breathing.

'*Be* the breathing,' advises Elaine. 'Not to think but to *be* is the secret of Zen ... As we advance in the awareness-of-being, and sharpen our breath awareness, stillness advances and a certain equanimity takes over. Very soon we feel better on the days we sit, and more scattered if, for some reason or other, we cannot meditate. The therapeutic effects of mature sitting are well known. Our dissipated energies gradually become more unified and we really start to gain some control over our superactive mind. Tensions are released, nerves become relaxed, and our physical health generally improves. Emotions are sensitized and the will strengthened. We begin to experience a kind of inner balance and gradually dryness, rigidity, hang-ups, prejudices and egotism melt and give way to compassion, serenity, egolessness and social concern. This is transformation indeed, although it does not happen the week after we start sitting. It is a life-long endeavour.'

Zen Buddhism is based, as most people know, on the words and life of the Buddha, the Indian prince who lived 2,500 years ago. He belonged to the Shakya clan and Buddhists usually give him the name of Shakyamuni. When he attained his awakening, or enlightenment, he was still a young man in his thirties and he lived and taught for many years afterwards. It is said that just after his awakening he uttered the word tathagata. Literally it means 'just comes, just goes'. Elaine says 'it denotes the state of perfection. Everything just as it comes and goes is perfect. Whatever the phenomenal limitation, the Essential is without blemish. Although, it is with considerable dissatisfaction that I use a word like "perfect" because it is usually judgemental and dichotomizing in the sense that it presupposes its opposite, "imperfect". Zen has to do with the world of non-duality, which transcends "perfect" and "imperfect".

'In Buddhist temples, one frequently sees a statue of Shakyamuni emerging from his experience [of awakening] and reaching down as though to touch the earth. This signifies his desire to return to the phenomenal world where suffering abounds. As the result of his experience he was compelled to go out to people and help them shed the shackles keeping them bound, which he found to be the cause of suffering. Shakyamuni subsequently spent the next forty-two years in this kind of service to people.

'And that is what Zen is all about. Experiencing the tathagata of the universe and then responding appropriately to our world and its violence and injustice and poverty and pollution. Shakyamuni did not just sit. His experience [of awakening] seemed to propel him into action for others. Yamada Roshi used to say if you cannot sympathize with another, there is no awakening. Experience [of enlightenment] realizes itself in involvement. Having found peace, we give peace. Social justice and sustainable development cannot happen on the intellectual level only, or by an act of the will. They must evolve from a deeper space.

'So when we step into the zendo, we are determined to reach that space. We leave all our learning and accomplishments as well as troubles and worries at the door. We put ourselves humbly but confidently and with great personal determination in the hands of a qualified teacher. Gradually, we experience the unifying process of Zen practice, and the benefits that accrue from it.

'And then, as Yamada Roshi used to say, when all things are ready, perhaps at a time least expected, you will break through the barrier and "shake the earth and astonish the heavens". You will find that heaven is not beyond the clouds at all, and God is closer than you are to yourself. Or, in the words of Zen master Hakuin: "This very place is the Lotus Land, this very body the Buddha." You will discover through personal experience that contemplation is indeed the hidden pearl of great price. I urge you to be most faithful to your daily sitting. One day it will pay joyful dividends.'

In 1976, fifteen years after she first arrived in Japan, Elaine was asked by the oriental Bishops to go to the Philippines. The Bishops had become well aware that Asia's spiritual values were breaking down and that oriental Christians were not doing well in their prayer life. They decided to go back to the prayer forms that were in the tradition of the great oriental religions and to encourage the establishment of ashrams and zendos. Since 1965 when the Vatican Council had changed the Church from a position of inflexibility to one of respect – that God had started all the great world religions – missionaries were no longer sent out to baptize but to learn the special ray of truth in the religion of the host country. When Elaine went to Manila it was not long before she was asked by the Cardinal there to start a zendo and to teach the way of Zen – for the Catholic Church. This was a most exciting challenge. Yamada Roshi gave his complete approval and came to Manila for the opening of the zendo. He had given Elaine a Japanese name when she received transmission from him: Ko-un Ang. Ang is a feminine suffix which means hermitage, 'un' means cloud and 'Ko' means light. But it was felt that the largely Catholic people of the Philippines would not easily accept a western nun with the title of roshi and a Japanese name. It would be better to let herself be known as Sister Elaine, and so she has remained to this day.

The years in Manila began to pass and the zendo flourished. But President Marcos was in power and stories circulated about the persecution and imprisonment of dissidents. One famous dissident was picked up and tortured for ten days. When the torture stopped and he recovered consciousness in his prison cell, he knew he needed help. His friends brought him books and among them was the yearly diary from the zendo. He then got word through the underground to Sister Elaine asking if she would teach him in prison. Elaine's phone was tapped and the message was a strange one. She knew that the army, the police and the Intelligence were Marcos's people – or, as she puts it, partners in crime – so she felt the situation was fraught with danger. She told the telephone caller to come to speak to her in person and then learnt that the dissident, Morales, had received an award, two years earlier, as the most promising young Philippino.

Elaine decided she must help him. But her own disciples might be in danger for they had often been picked up and questioned. They had been told by the questioners: 'We're following that nun. She makes you sit on the floor facing the wall! What kind of a nun is that? And she doesn't wear a habit. You must be careful of nuns that don't wear habits.' So Elaine knew that she had to act with immense caution. She decided the wisest move would be to go to the Canadian Embassy. She asked for the Ambassador. He was a kindly, humorous man who had just received a box of fruit cake from Canada, so they drank tea and ate cake together.

'What do you want?' he asked. She told him.

He looked at her and then said, 'If you go in to see Morales, you'll be deported before the end of the week.'

She said, 'I know. That's why I'm here.'

'I think you'd better decide not to go.'

'No, that decision's made,' she replied. 'I'm going. But you're in a position where you might be able to help me so that I won't get deported.'

Again he looked at her for a while. Then he said, 'Excuse me,' and left the room. He came back with the First Consul and said, 'We both know Morales very well. We feel that he is the big hope for this country in the future and we're going to help you. A general owes us a favour. He was here last week asking if his daughter could get into a Canadian university and we arranged it for him.'

He picked up the phone. He got through to the general and said, 'General, you owe me one. I've got a Canadian nun here who's been asked by Morales to teach him Zen in prison. I want her safety assured.'

'You have it,' replied the general.

Every Friday for the next four years Elaine visited Morales. It was not long before she had established a proper zendo in the prison. Morales wanted his friends in prison to take part and when he asked the prison governor, a colonel, if they could, the colonel said, 'Yes, and I'll sit in on it too.' So Elaine scrubbed out a room and put newspapers down. She gave her first teisho to ten political prisoners and the colonel. Just outside was the firing range and she found it ironic that she should talk of Zen and silence to the accompaniment of gunfire.

The general kept his word and she was not molested, although the guards were always hostile and constantly accused her of bringing things in from the underground and passing on information and of not teaching Zen at all. But there was nothing they could do and every week she spent four hours in the prison. First they would sit for half an hour, then she would give a talk. After that, she would go into a small adjacent room and each prisoner would come in for a private interview with her. 'I had the wonderful experience of seeing this man Morales and his companion detainees change from an angry, tense, enervated and incapacitated group to a relaxed, sociable, energized and effective team. The change was illustrated by the arrangement of their shoes.

'When I first went to the prison and saw its hostile environment, I decided to dispense with the hundred or so regulations attending a meditation centre. One of the rules is to leave your shoes neatly in a row. The first day I happened to look up from my cushion during a talk and saw a mass of rubber slippers. What a mess!

'I desisted from saying anything, and it was not until about six months later, I noticed all the slippers perfectly lined up by the side of the wall. I burst out laughing, and told the detainees about their change of habit. Their quick reply was, "It's not just our shoes. You should see what's happening to the rest of our lives." How was this accomplished? you may ask. I was simply teaching them the value and use of silence. Silencing the body and silencing the mind and regulating our own healing breath. Meditation is as simple and difficult as that.'

Three of the prisoners experienced kensho, including Morales himself, and this gave Elaine great joy.

At last the revolution took place, Marcos was deposed, and the political prisoners were freed. A new senate was to be formed and Morales stood for it. A journalist asked him what had been the peak experience of his life and Morales replied, 'My kensho experience in prison.'

Those years formed the beginning of Elaine's work with prisoners. Eventually she left Manila and is now in England, where she is the Director of the Prison Phoenix Trust in Oxford. This Trust works to help prisoners turn their imprisonment into a space to grow and to use their cells as places of spiritual retreat. Being shut in a cell for much of the day can be an opportunity for change. What can be done is to learn to sit, to breathe, to use the body properly in yoga, and these are methods which all the major religions have used for centuries to increase spiritual awareness and compassion.

Over three thousand prisoners are now in touch with the Trust, news of it having spread almost entirely by word of mouth between prisoners. They have come to see that ordinary life itself can be a prison unless you can begin to accept responsibility for yourself. They take responsibility for their past and future actions instead of just 'doing time'. 'I guess I'm in search of access to what life is really about,' says one. 'I thought I knew it all and now realize that I've spent a whole lifetime sleeping.'

Elaine and her volunteer staff correspond with men and women in prisons, young offender institutions and secure hospitals. They arrange for books, cassettes and videos to be sent, and for visits from meditation and yoga teachers, psychologists and stress management experts. Elaine has a lot of hope for the prisoners and is excited about the work. 'I can't teach them all Zen,' she says, 'but I can teach silencing the mind with simple breath awareness.'

She is however able to teach Zen in Oxford itself and a number of people there are becoming Zen practitioners. Now, looking back, she says, 'I started Zen to know the Japanese people better, I continued it as a personal discipline in the development of my own spirituality, and finally chose it as my service to others.'

Although Elaine has now lived a long life in Zen, she never forgets that she is a Catholic nun. At the end of her book *Teaching Zen to Christians* she explains to a doubtful questioner how she sees the two paths merging in her practice.

The questioner asks: 'As a Christian, you believe that God is a person, don't you?'

Elaine replies: 'Yes, I believe God is person but since I have some fear of that word "believe" and the way it is sometimes used today, I would also like to say that I have experienced God as person.'

Q: 'But I understand the mystical experience of kensho is not of God as person. Did you find that to be so in your kensho?'

E: 'I would articulate kensho as an experience of the power of God, and yes that is non-personal.'

Q: 'Well, isn't that a problem for you?'

E: 'Not really. The part of the paradigm change we have already experienced has brought us out of "either–or" into the "both–and" category. The Church has always taught that God is both transcendent and immanent, but somehow the former seemed to dominate in our religion. Now I feel more spiritually balanced.'

Q: 'So you can be both Christian and Buddhist?'

E: 'Now you're back into religions!'

Q: 'Well, where are you?'

E: 'I'm in the field of what we call spirituality. My spirituality is a combination of western Christianity which teaches me to relate to God who is transcendent, and oriental spirituality which teaches me to commune with the immanent God . . . When I became a sister, I found I sometimes easily tired of words and feelings in prayer, and sought for a teacher in what we call contemplative prayer, not using words or feeling. It was not until I came to the Orient that I found one, and to my delight and surprise, I realized that the Oriental Way is all about the Immanent God, with whom all creation is ONE and therefore not in a position of relationship but of communion. For me it is not "either–or" but "both–and" and I am very grateful for this.'

Q: 'But doesn't the oppressive masculinity of the Christian God get to you?'

E: 'As you probably know, the matrix of Christianity is Judaism, which has always been strongly masculine. And being a woman in the world and of this time and place, I am more comfortable with the non-sexist terminology. God is not masculine, not feminine and both. You might be interested to know that our community recites the ancient Hebraic psalms using *inclusive* terminology. And the feminine issue is one of our concerns.'

Elaine is privately shocked by the antagonism to women in western religion, but she sees it as part of a much greater problem – that of the separation between ego and the world, between subject and object, a separation which has become the basis of all our perception. Because we normally experience ourselves as separate from the world we live in, even estranged from it, we lose touch with our real nature and the result is a sick society and a threatened world. Seeing ourselves in opposition to the world engenders isolation and fear.

She believes that a different perception of the world is possible and that the way of Zen can bring this about. She herself, as her sitting deepened and matured, saw things differently in a quite literal sense. 'Perhaps the best articulation is that we get glimpses, very fleetingly and incompletely, but still glimpses of the Truth that all phenomena are empty and the other and I are not separate.' Other people also have found a marked change in their perception of everything about them as they came in contact with the Zen path.

An English teacher, with a new awareness, said, 'There was a blackbird in the garden, and it was as though there had never been a blackbird before. All my inner turmoil melted away and I felt full of clarity and indescribable peace. I seemed at one with everything around me and saw people with judgement suspended, so that they seemed perfect in themselves.'

Flora Courtois in her book *An Experience of Enlightenment* tells us: 'The small pale green desk at which I'd been so thoughtlessly gazing had totally and radically changed. It appeared now with a clarity, a depth of three-dimensionality, a freshness I had never imagined possible. At the same time, in a way that is utterly indescribable, all my questions and doubts were gone as effortlessly as chaff in the wind. I knew everything and all at once, yet not in the sense that I had ever known anything before.

'This new kind of knowing was so pure and unadorned, so delicate, that nothing in the language of my past could express it. Neither sense nor feeling nor imagination contained it yet all were contained in it. In some indefinable way I knew with absolute certainty the changeless unity and harmony of the universe and the inseparability of all seeming opposites.'

. . . 'Of all the changes, the one that seemed to me in some mysterious way to be the key to everything else was the change in vision. It was as if some inner eye, some ancient centre of awareness, which extended equally and at once and in all directions without limit and which had been there all along had been restored. This inner vision seemed to be anchored in infinity in a way that was detached from immediate sight and yet at the same time had a profound effect on sight.'

To see 'the changeless unity and harmony of the universe and the inseparability of all seeming opposites' is exactly what Elaine feels the Zen path can accomplish through its ability to bring people to such an altered perception: 'As you probably know, the whole world is in the midst of a great change; a new paradigm is evolving, a different world view . . . and many say that one of its characteristics will be that we will perceive differently. Father Lassalle has predicted that the new perception will be the Zen way of mystical perception.'

She sees the aim of Zen as the personalization, or actualization, of such perception throughout the entire being and in all daily activities.

'To come to it [perception] is not very difficult. For some people, only one sesshin is necessary. But to accomplish our ultimate personality is very difficult indeed, and requires a long period of time. The experience itself is only the entrance. The completion is to personalize what we came to realize at the moment of awakening. And then, after washing away all the glitter and ecstasy, the truly great Zen people are not different externally from other human beings. Through zazen and kensho you don't become a special person or a strange person, or an eccentric and esoteric character. You become a normal person, a real person, and as far as possible a true human being . . .

'In his teisho at the Kamakura Zendo, Yamada Roshi often referred to throwing away the experience, discarding it completely, and proceeding to the market place. He always taught that virtue rises in the heart, and that the wisdom of kensho inevitably brings a corresponding impulse to compassion . . . Considering our many problems today, this happening and process is precisely what is needed to restore harmony in the universe, and to make Earth a nourishing environmental home for ourselves and our children.

'And our practice remains just sitting . . . You may be very good at it, for we occasionally find a beginner for whom it is natural. After getting yourself settled on the cushion, count the breath. Then, if you want to, you can stop the counting and just follow the breath. Just that. Keep trying.'

Iris Murdoch

' "Happiness," said Willy, "is a matter of one's most ordinary everyday mode of consciousness being busy and lively and unconcerned with self. To be damned is for one's ordinary everyday mode of consciousness to be unremitting agonizing preoccupation with self." '

Our sense of the sacred can take many forms. For Iris it exists in selflessness, goodness, the nature turning outwards to embrace the world just as it is in all its ordinariness.

How dull this can sound until one actually does it! The New Age, in contrast, is filled with spiritual fireworks, states of mind that can transport one to other worlds, mystical paths that can lead to vast and colourful experiences. But Iris talks of reality and clarity, of seeing real things in the sunlight with an awakened mind, of the world revealed as so beautiful that the powerful ego with all its desires and shadows is vanquished – even if only for a short time, because the light can dazzle. But that short seeing helps one to know truth in a new way and to see the difference between the real and the unreal in the clear light of reality itself.

In Iris's play *Acastos*, Acastos asks Plato if knowing the truth is similar to really understanding mathematics. Plato replies: 'Yes, like when you *really* understand anything – and that's *difficult* – I don't just mean slick cleverness, I mean something which shakes the whole soul and opens it out into some huge brightness and this is love too, when we love real things and see them distinctly in a clear light . . . And when we begin to know and find out, it's wonderful, it's like remembering, as if we were coming home to a spiritual world where we really belong.'

Loving real things, as Iris's Plato says, brings true wisdom; and all the matters that are difficult to understand somehow come together so that the connections can be seen. Real wisdom – goodness and clarity – brings into being a wonderful freedom. Such freedom is different in kind from the way in which most people understand the word because it's not just intellectual understanding, it's seeing all things in the light of the sun and then 'seeing the sun itself – and that's goodness – and joy –'

Theologians might want to use the term God rather than the sun but Iris herself does not believe in a personal God and would not find it to be an accurate description. Her freedom is the freedom to go forth and love things without putting them in categories such as religion or morality. Being 'in love' with good is a phrase that her Plato uses and that way of being passionately concerned is something about which she feels strongly.

'Concern about everything – with one's environment, with people, with one's thoughts and so on – there should be an element of passion. I think that love and passion must belong in all our activities, in writing and thinking and philosophy. It is fundamental. Some people might come from Mars and say: "Oh, we don't have passion. We're very clever and kind to our people and everything works well on our planet." But something would be missing if there wasn't this passionate aspect too. It's something which comes out of the soul and belongs with forgiveness and every sort of activity which goes to the putting together of a human being. However careful or clever or profound people are, even in what they do in caring for other people, if their caring has not got that love, if it's cold, then something is missing.'

Love is an energy, Iris says, and it is essential that we should not neglect it but use it by loving people, learning things and looking at things. It's not an abstract quality, not just one choice among others, but in a sense it is the whole of the 'way'. To love is to be *here*, not retiring from the world but discovering the real world – the world as it really is.

But learning things and really looking at the world often comes more easily to us than loving other people – that is much more difficult and yet it is much more important. We seem to be naturally good at loving beauty ('the only spiritual thing we love by instinct') and bad at loving people. But if we see love as an energy we can change ourselves: 'The soul is a huge vast place and lots of it is dark, and it's full of energy and power, and this can be bad, but it *can* be good, and that's the *work*, to change bad energy into good, when we desire good things and are attracted magnetically to them –'

The work of transformation, of learning to look, to be, to love, belongs, many might feel, to religion. But what, nowadays, is religion? Iris herself, although brought up an Anglican, is very attracted to Buddhism. She is also attracted to the Quakers and many of her family are Quakers. She does not feel herself to be a religious person in any conventional sense, but she is sure that goodness and selflessness exist and that they matter absolutely: 'We can lose God but we can't lose good.' The quality of goodness shouldn't be personalized into a God, she feels. We can't have dialogues with it, it won't reward us. It is the certainty that comes to us, perhaps at times of deep stress, that in spite of all the depravity and wretchedness there really is goodness and it matters absolutely.

Iris's Plato tells us that people instinctively know the reality and absoluteness of good and when they choose false goods they really know they're false. To love good and to act in accordance with that love is the basis of true religion and morality. Wanting good, but desiring other things more, turns the activity into duty.

Religion, in our materialistic world, is an exotic activity set aside from life, but in varying degrees it has perhaps always been so, at least in the West. We can think of the Middle Ages, when the Inquisition defended the 'pure faith' and God was debated everywhere, as a time when religion was powerful. But was it not the tradition rather than the spirit which was so strong, for the mystics were still far and few between and often persecuted? Religion seems to consist mostly – at least in history – of certain picturesque traditions expressed in hallowed rituals, symbols and familiar pictures, and clung to by people who need the security of a traditional life.

But nowadays such traditions have largely lost their ancient power. The stories and symbols have turned into mythology and we question the existence of the old God. And so religion comes to be ignored because many still think of it in the old outgrown way. Yet religion should mean spiritual change, not clinging to old myths. Iris's Socrates suggests that perhaps the whole concept of mythology is breaking up, as well as religion. But Plato replies that if so, it is a good thing and he thinks of mythology as sets of false stories. Human life is coherent enough, it doesn't need mythology. 'There are,' he says, 'lots of ways of talking about the – absolute – however you put it, with *true* images, *true* pointers, natural – sacraments –'

And here we come to the heart of Iris's view of the sacred: the true, the natural, the real. 'For what is real and true look at these stones, this bread, the spring of water, those sea waves, this horizon with its pure untroubled line. Only perceive purely and the spiritual and the material world vibrate as one. The power that saves is infinitely simple and infinitely close at hand.'

We need a certain way of perception and a great humbling of our usual sensation-seeking ego if we are to find that particular experience of blessedness when spirit and matter become one. The humbling of the ego is an essential first step and practices abound, for instance in Buddhism, to help one loosen its grip. But without even going as far as Buddhism it is possible to lessen the *feeling* of self simply by considering what we are and what our situation is. There is something utterly mysterious, beyond all reach of our knowledge, in the fact that we are alive at all. It is very paradoxical that objects made of such unpromising material as ourselves could be self-conscious and know that there is a limit to our understanding, a strange edge to our consciousness – death – beyond which we cannot go. Western religion would like to insert God beyond that edge and see some sort of personal purpose in our existence. But egoism tends to get inserted with that viewpoint and, if we are really humble, it is surely spiritual enough to be awe-struck by the impenetrable nature of being conscious at all, of being here, and of knowing that we are here, without going any further? If we are willing to be enthusiastically unknowing, to be wordless, dumb-struck at the amazing mystery of the world in all its beingness and to be satisfied with our wonder, we may find ourselves in a state of humble grace. It is when we start to look for explanations of the Mystery that we fall from grace. Most theology does seem to be an attempt to go beyond the Mystery, the blessed unknowing, to a state of pseudo-knowing, of imagined hypotheses to account for the fact that we don't know how it is that we have come to exist.

It is this besmirching theology of guesswork and hypothesis that, when it is believed to be true after the manner of ordinary truths, is responsible for religious persecution. Iris, who was born in Dublin and considers herself Irish, has strong feelings about the wretched situation religion has brought about in Ireland. But although Christianity can show a dark and confused side, and she herself finds Buddhism a more enlightened way of seeing the world, she would not like to lose the idea of Christ as an ideal of selflessness. 'A literal personal God and the divinity of Christ and life after death – these things I don't believe in. But to keep the idea of Christ is, I think, very important. Christ meant much to me when I was a girl and still means much to me. I've never really felt detached from the feeling. But to change the figure of Christ into an icon, as it were, without losing the whole thing is very difficult.'

A refreshed conception of transcendence is needful, she thinks: 'To realize that one is not the master of one's own soul, that there is something higher and that there's something which is continuously with one. Perhaps transcendence is not a very useful word because people might not like it or understand it, but it's to do with getting a kind of vision or insight about what it would be like to be selfless.'

To realize that we are not masters of our own soul is, again, a real humbler. But if we think for only a moment we must know how true that is. We have eyes, so we think we see things but the eyes see whether we order them to or not. We have ears, so we hear sounds but whether we want to hear them or not is beyond our control. We can't conquer sleep even if we try to stay awake; we can't conquer death even if we try to stay alive. Ultimately our human nature is nothing but the function of nature itself. If we see these facts as reductionist – reducing all humanity to nothing – then we will be miserable. But if we see them as magnificent evidence of a majestically mysterious cosmos of which we are expressions, and of which we are a part but not the master – we may, even if only for an instant, suddenly feel a sense of true being.

The perception in which we see the spiritual and material 'vibrating as one' is not, for Iris, anything to be cultivated that is out of the ordinary. 'I see no need for a dramatic voluntarist "way" to be pressed upon us by theologians. The ordinary way is the way. It is not in that sense theology, and the "mysticism" involved is an accessible experience.'

That accessible experience is indeed the basis of a certain modern mysticism. Evelyn Underhill, an English mystic of this century, advises a training of our faculties and a brightening of our languid and often indifferent consciousness, a freedom from the bondage of appearance, a turning of attention to new dimensions and levels. 'This amount of mystical perception – this "ordinary contemplation" – is possible to all men; without it they are not wholly conscious, nor wholly alive.'

And Frederick Franck, a Zen artist, says: 'When I *see*, suddenly I am all eyes, I forget this Me, am liberated from it and dive into the reality of what confronts me, become part of it, participate in it. I no longer label, no longer choose . . . I believe that in *seeing* there is a way of focusing attention until it turns into contemplation and from there to the inexpressible fullness where the split between the seer and what is seen is obliterated.'

The 'ordinary way' for Iris means a profound empathy, a 'being with' all natural things – rocks and branches, the wind, the sea and animals. This is one factor in her liking for Zen Buddhism, for Zen refuses to dislodge earth from heaven and believes that it's possible to see all 'the ten thousand things' as transparent to their original Source. Her many novels reflect her very deep 'devotion' to existence. She feels herself into people and situations in such a way that it seems she has not created them but has described living people. Such writing has earned her world recognition and the bestowal of many honours, including Dame of the British Empire.

Her novels are full of emotional turbulence as people wrestle with their longings to love, to possess and to renounce. But Iris herself appears to have lived serenely, at least since her marriage to a fellow professor in 1956. Her life and work have centred round Oxford from her youth and she considers herself a philosopher first and foremost.

In her novels philosophy appears under various guises. Love, for instance, is the main theme as it is for most novels, but Iris's love is rarely simple although often it is movingly profound: 'Realizing that one is in love with someone in whom one has long been interested is a curious process. What can it be said to consist of? Each human being swims within a sea of faint suggestive imagery. It is this web of pressures, currents and suggestions, something often so much less definite than pictures, which ties our fugitive present to our past and future, composing the globe of consciousness. We think with our body, with its yearnings and its shrinkings and its ghostly walkings.'

In *The Nice and the Good* a woman called Mary finds she is suddenly in love with someone she has known for a long time. She had thought she was in love with someone else but now realizes she was not. 'No, she had not been in love with Willy. She had loved Willy with her careful anxious mind and with her fretful fingertips. She had not thus adored him with her whole thought-body, her whole being of yearning. She had not been content to be for him simply herself and a woman. This was the old, the unmistakable state of being in love which she had imagined she would never experience again.'

But being in love in such a happy fashion is not the only sort of loving that Iris describes. In *The Sea, The Sea* the main character, Charles, is in love in an obsessive way that destroys his sense of reality and the book is an extraordinary contrast between the vastness of the sea and the narrowness of his vision. He is no longer young and the girl he had loved in his youth is his own age, with grey hair and a plump figure. Meeting her again, he is determined to love her as he did before and to overcome all the facts of her present existence, even of her husband. His love is thus completely blind and, because of this, destructive. He imprisons her but in the end has to let her free and gradually come to terms with his obsession.

When did I begin to relax my hold upon Hartley, or rather upon her image, her double, the Hartley of my mind? Have I relaxed my hold, did it happen before, or is it only happening now, when I can look back over the summer and see my acts and thoughts as those of a madman? I remember Rosina saying to me that her desire for me was made of jealousy, resentment, anger, not love. Was the same true of my desire for Hartley? . . . Whatever the cause, it is now clear that something is over. My new, my second love for her, my second 'innings', seemed at its height a thing sublime, even without illusion, when I had seen her as so pitiful, so broken, and yet as something which I could cherish, something which I could hold and be held by, and which would be a source of light even if I were to lose her utterly. What has become of that light now? It has gone and was at best a flickering flame seen in a marsh, and my great 'illumination' a kind of nonsense. She is gone, she is nothing for me, she no longer exists, and after all I fought for a phantom Helen.

To read an Iris Murdoch novel is to become enwrapped in intensely personal questions and situations which yet have an ultimate dimension to them. The problems of the world are tackled in the light of a just and loving detachment. Nothing is left out for no character is simple, all are complex and evil is present with good, hate with love, physical attack with physical adoration. Through the tangle of different voices, each one convincing in its own way, we find glimpses of Iris's own ideas and preferences and dislikes.

She does not like, for instance, the misuse of occult powers. In *The Nice and the Good* Ducane, a good man, has to search through a room where a now-dead colleague, Radeechy, had conducted some occult experiments:

It's the dreariness of it, thought Ducane, that stupefies. This evil is dreary, it's something shut in and small, dust falling upon cobwebs, a bloodstain upon the garment, a heap of dead birds in a packing case. Whatever it was that Radeechy had so assiduously courted and attracted to himself, and which had breathed upon him, squirted over him that odour of decay, had no intensity or grandeur. These were but small powers, graceless and bedraggled. Yet could not evil damn a man, was there no blackness enough to kill a human soul? It is in me, thought Ducane . . . The evil is in me. There are demons and powers outside us, Radeechy played with them, but they are pygmy things. The great evil, the real evil, is inside myself. It is I who am Lucifer . . . Perhaps there were spirits, perhaps there were evil spirits, but they were little things. The great evil, the dreadful evil, that which made war and slavery and all man's inhumanity to man lay in the cool self-justifying ruthless selfishness of quite ordinary people, such as himself.

Yet although Iris might have a strong distaste for meddlings with bad spirits, she enjoys the *frisson* caused by the totally unexpected. In *The Nice and the Good* a pair of young twins who have the freedom of the seashore to wander in frequently see a flying saucer, although nobody believes them or indeed listens to them:

The twins lay on the clifftop up above Gunnar's Cave. The beautiful flying saucer, spinning like a huge noiseless top, hovered in the air not far away from them, a little higher up, over the sea, in a place where they had often seen it come before. The shallow metal dome glowed with a light which seemed to emanate from itself and owe nothing to the sun, and about the slim tapering outer extremity a thin line of lambent blue flame rippled and leapt. It was difficult to discern the size of the saucer, which seemed to inhabit a space of its own, as if it were inserted or pocketed in a dimension to which it did not quite belong. In some way it defeated the attempt of the human eye to estimate and measure. It hovered in its own element, in its own silence, indubitably physical, indubitably present and yet other. Then, as the children watched, it tilted slightly, and with that movement which they could never confidently interpret either as speed or as some sort of dematerializing or actual vanishing, it was gone.

The brilliance of such a description almost suggests that Iris has seen such an object, for there is not just the physical description but a sense that she is there and deeply involved with what she sees. But the same feeling that she is describing something real and known occurs with a sea monster in *The Sea, The Sea* (when we realize she was *not* present) and with an adolescent girl's – Moy's – ability to move objects without touching them in *The Green Knight*. Moy is a sensitive girl, deeply aware of creatures and objects, and of her responsibility for them:

Every day she rescued the snail or slug or worm from the pavement where it might be stepped on, the spider from the bath where it was imprisoned, the tiniest almost invisible creatures who were in some wrong place where they might starve or be crushed. She was the one too who always found things which were lost in the house. But was this not something fruitless or even bad? How did she know what little living creatures, and even *things*, wanted her to do? The whole world was a jumble of mysterious destinies. Did the stones who were picked up by humans and taken into their houses *mind*, did they dislike being inside a house, dry, gathering dust, missing the open air, the rain, perhaps the company of other stones?

Such reflections seem very close to Iris's heart, and indeed stones feature in several of her books. In her own drawing-room she keeps a number of interesting stones on a centre table. But the way in

27

which stones move of themselves for Moy is an imaginative leap of Iris's and reflects the way in which she treats such supernatural manifestations as natural extensions of the known world – as once fairies and elves were 'seen', or the god Odin riding through the night sky.

She turned in time to see something moving upon the shelf, a piece of grey speckled granite had shifted from its place. Moy was used to being called 'fey', not attaching much meaning to the word. Lately however she had developed a curious power, that of making small objects move simply by looking at them with a certain concentration. She had discovered this talent by accident, she even knew a scientific name for it, *telekinesis*. The fact that it had this impressive name might have served as a reassurance since it implied that other people had it too. However it frightened Moy and she kept it secret. What had just happened alarmed her even more. So now things could move on their own, perhaps whenever they wished?

Iris concedes the possibility through another character in *The Green Knight* that we may be surrounded by beings, heavenly or demonic, for whom we have no concepts and who are therefore invisible: 'as if something huge and strange has shot up in our midst and we simply cannot conceptualize it and so we imagine that it isn't there, like the New Zealand natives who could not conceptualize Captain Cook's ship and simply ignored it'.

The Green Knight also brings into prominence Iris's delight in the idea of the avatar or selfless person. Many of her novels pivot around an almost magical character who 'arrives'. Often he has been known before and then lost sight of, but sometimes he is new to everybody as is the case of Peter Mir in *The Green Knight*. Mir whose name is Russian and means several things – rock, world and peace – is nearly killed by a blow to the head and loses his memory or, rather, his memory of one very important thing in his life, which he spends most of the novel searching for. Eventually a burst of light reveals what he has lost, which is the concept of God and transcendence. But Mir is by no means an all-white character and it is part of Iris's concern with the good that she can see the natural muddle of humanity and events. Although Mir, as a warm, caring 'inspired' person, is opposed to Lucas (the one who nearly murdered him), who is dark, cold and clear, the opposition is not entirely between good and evil, for Lucas is more realistic than anyone else in the book, although infinitely more selfish.

Other of her novels have reflected the opposition between warmth and light and cold and dark, but often the 'evil' person or act opens up a gap in the fabric of the characters' lives through which goodness spreads. Iris has attended to the way in which paradoxically one quality can lead to its opposite, so that life is never a straightforward battle between good and bad but is more like the Buddhist concept of 'ignorance of the good' when, as ignorance is replaced by understanding, new values are revealed. Indeed 'bad' and 'good' are never abstract points to Iris but are always embodied as human qualities. It is as though we are all moving in various preordained ways according to who we are but then the very walls of our existence begin to melt and change as though some higher but yet still natural force were intervening. So there is always hope, we are never quite abandoned to mechanical existence. 'You have a healing substance in your own body and soul, it is called courage.' But we must recognize the revelation when it comes and Iris sees such essential acknowledgement as needing not only courage but also the discipline of strict attention – very much a Buddhist practice.

Such attention is undoubtedly Iris's 'way' and it is not only concerned with finding revelation but also with expressing her warm but detached love for all that exists. She is wonderfully lucid in her descriptions of the natural world, especially of animals – who are often much nicer than humans and certainly more unselfish. A dog such as Anax in *The Green Knight* often shows up the humans as lesser and more mixed-up beings than himself.

Anax [who had been discarded by his master] grieved and waited, aware that his kind captors were careful not to let him stray. Sometimes he pretended to be happy, sometimes, quite accidentally, he was happy because for an instant he forgot, and then remembering was a greater grief. He did not reflect upon any reason why he had been deprived of the one he loved and to whom he had given his life. He knew simply that there was no other. He did not believe that his master rejected him or found him unworthy, indeed he could not imagine this. Nor did he imagine that his master might be dead, since Anax could not conceive of death. He felt only the painful unnatural severance from the loved one and the utterly poisoned wrongness of the world while the severance lasted.

Anax held no grudges and when his master did eventually reclaim him, his delight contained no hint of reproach or forgiveness, although forgiveness is a vital theme in Iris's novels. In *The Nice and the Good* she makes the point that:

All we can do is constantly to notice when we begin to act badly, to check ourselves, to go back, to coax our weakness and inspire our strength, to call upon the names of virtues of which we know perhaps only the names. We are not good people, and the best we can hope for is to be gentle, to forgive each other and to forgive the past, to be forgiven ourselves and to accept this forgiveness, and to return again to the beautiful unexpected strangeness of the world.

Quite often it seems as though an animal – a dog like Anax – is the avatar in Iris's books. But Iris does have a belief that people are born who can manifest pure love and selflessness, such as the Buddha or Christ: 'The concept of the avatar I would certainly want to survive because I think there are people who are very remarkable, purely good and so on.' And in *Metaphysics as a Guide to Morals* she remarks: 'Great saints and avatars may, in this age too and onward, live with us as mysteries, as mythical mystical exemplars and saviours. The *truth*, the *light* which they bestow "floats free" from contingent detail and is not at the mercy of history.'

To reach such a state of selflessness is undoubtedly Iris's goal, but one that she feels is far off for herself: 'I've had luck simply in seeing good examples – whether I adopted them or not is another matter. You know, I'm not elevated at all. I'm just lucky to have had guidance when I was young. There's a very large space between me in my ordinariness and the really exalted figures – I'm even thinking of my Quaker connections who were more genuinely selfless.'

But perhaps Iris has had luck in other ways too, and has paid attention and taken proper advantage of it, putting it to work in the world. She was born in 1919, the only and much beloved child of Protestant and Catholic Irish parents. The family, whom she has called 'a perfect trinity', moved from Dublin to London when she was a year old – a decision which was hers, she believes! She went to a famous boarding-school, Badminton, and from there to Somerville College in Oxford where she continued as a happy studious girl. One of her contemporaries remembered that everybody fell in love with Iris at Oxford. After working with the Treasury in London and with the United Nations in Belgium and Austria, she went to Paris when the war was ended. This was the time of Sartre and the Existentialists but Iris, although she knew Sartre, remembers the singer Edith Piaf better.

After Paris she studied philosophy at Cambridge (perhaps the Existentialists *did* have an effect) and then returned to Oxford as a Fellow of St Anne's. Her husband, John Bayley, famously fell in love with her when he saw her cycling past his window. Now they live in North Oxford, in a quiet road where houses are large and gardens full of trees. But Iris's house is not very big and she and her husband live modestly, even frugally – except for books. They cover the walls and are piled on floors. Where there are no books, there are paintings and on the tops of bookcases are statues, including a fine reclining Buddha.

Iris's simple life style is demonstrated by the fact that although she receives hundreds of letters she answers each one herself with warmth and thoughtfulness and also with remarkable promptness. Her husband does the cooking, which is a relief to Iris, for although her accounts of meals in her novels are famous she is not much good at preparing them.

Although her fiction is the medium in which her ideas become people and animals and seascapes, Iris really prefers to be thought of as a philosopher. Her most recent philosophical book *Metaphysics as a Guide to Morals* is a true approach to the sacred because it is about the difference between analytic and moral ways of thinking, how these have become separated in our thought, and hence about the spiritual vacuum in which we find ourselves. Was there ever a wholeness, a unity of being which we have lost? Iris finds reflections of it in art and religion but sets out to show that we can never finally know what reality is, the reality that lies behind appearance. It is the Mystery and philosophers err if they do not take it into account. Metaphysics, she believes, is to be justified as this process of pointing beyond.

'We speak of the veil of appearance. We know when we are being satisfied with superficial, illusory, lying pictures which distort and conceal reality . . . By looking at something, by *stopping* to look at it, we do not selfishly appropriate it, we understand it and let it be. We may too, in such looking, take the object as shadow, intuiting what is beyond it . . . Blind desire, of which lust is an image, reaches out to grasp and appropriate. Desire with vision looks first, and in approaching what is near is aware of what is far. Looking can be a kind of intelligent reverence.'

Does Iris have a spiritual 'way'? She replies no, she does not. 'I think I would rather not use the image. I'm not really on the way at all, a very ordinary personage.' Iris may not claim to have a way, may in fact disclaim it strongly because she feels that realization lies in the present moment rather than in a future 'goal', but she does nevertheless advocate certain practices of change and transformation.

'The fundamental value is truth . . . The world is not given to us "on a plate", it is given to us as a creative task. It is impossible to banish morality from this picture. We *work*, using or failing to use our honesty, our courage, our truthful imagination, at the interpretation of what is present to us, as we of necessity shape it and "make something of it". We help it to be. We work at the meeting point where we deal with a world which is other than ourselves. This transcendental barrier is more like a band than a line. Our ordinary consciousness is a deep continuous working of values, a *continuous present and presence* of perceptions, intuitions, images, feelings, desires, aversions, attachments. It is a matter of what we "see things as", what we let, or make, ourselves think about, how by innumerable movements we train our instincts and develop our habits and test our methods of verification.'

Iris believes we can shift to a different way of thinking by attending and perceiving without the interference of reflective thought: 'Should we not endeavour to see and attend to what surrounds and concerns us, because it is there and is interesting, beautiful, strange, worth experiencing and because it demands (and *needs*) our attention, rather than living in a vague haze of private anxiety and fantasy? . . . Alert, vivid experience, living in the present, can be celebrated as the higher hedonism, or as moral or "spiritual" attention.'

So the turning of the attention outwards is, to Iris, an essential mystical practice, but it needs effort.

'To silence and expel self, to contemplate and delineate nature with a clear eye, is not easy and demands a moral discipline . . . The appreciation of beauty in art and nature is not only (for all its difficulties) the easiest available spiritual exercise; it is also a completely adequate entry into the good life, since it is the checking of selfishness in the interest of seeing the real . . . This exercise of *detachment* is difficult and valuable whether the thing contemplated is a human being or the root of a tree or the vibrations of a colour or a sound . . . selfish concerns vanish, nothing exists except the things which are seen. Beauty is that which attracts this particular sort of unselfish attention. It is obvious here what is the role for the spectator, for the artist, of exactness and good vision: unsentimental, detached, unselfish, objective attention. It is also clear that in moral situations a similar exactness is called for. I would suggest that the authority of the Good seems to us something necessary because the realism (ability to perceive reality) required for goodness is a kind of intellectual ability to perceive what is true, which is automatically at the same time a suppression of self.'

It is important, Iris believes, that in the west we begin to take in ideas of religion without God and to learn to meditate as a religious exercise. 'There is, just as there used (with the old God) to be, a place of wisdom and calm to which we can remove ourselves. We can make our own rites and images, we can preserve the concept of holiness.' She finds Buddhism particularly helpful here: 'Sitting and breathing, which of course belongs to Buddhism and Hinduism, I think this is very important. It's *ipso facto* reverential. If people did learn to sit down or kneel down and breathe quietly – up to ten and so on – they might see the events of the day in a different perspective.'

In *Metaphysics as a Guide to Morals* she wonders if such religious practices can make people better:

Certainly it may make them more calm, more 'collected', less given to egoistic passions, in many ways more 'unselfish' . . . What about *love* as it is understood by Plato and in Christianity? Well, again, how can one say? What Christians call love may on closer inspection

33

appear to be shot with egoisms and delusions. Zen [Buddhism] may seem cold, yet Zen art lovingly portrays the tiny things of the world, the details, blithely existing without intelligibility; this too is moral training . . . Buddhism teaches respect and love for *all things*. This concerned attention implies or effects a removal from the usual egoistic fuzz of self-protective anxiety. One may be sure that those who observe stones and snails lovingly will also thus observe human beings, but such observation is a *way*, an act of respect for individuals, which is of itself a virtue and an image of virtue. The enlightened man returns to, that is, *discovers* the world.

She believes that many people leave their churches because their reason will not accept belief in the old God or saints and visions and revelations. Buddhism and Hinduism have avoided 'the awkward unique figure of the Judaeo-Christian god as Individual Person'. If there are many gods or icons it is possible to gain strength from these as sources of spiritual energy rather than as historical supernatural people.

Iris has a particular dislike of attempts to push God into history. 'If one does want to believe in what is "deep" in the form of the old God, then let this belief be kept mysterious and separated and pure, not mixed up with dubious history, or indeed with any history . . . The renewal of the holy and sacred is and can only be here and now, and is indeed still happening all the time.'

Practice, for Iris, would also include the possibility that we can save or cherish creation 'by lending a consciousness to nature'. We can do this by paying real attention to what we do with time.

. . . why do we have to wait for accidental experiences which may, if we are lucky, make us artists? Should we not attempt to turn most of our time from dead (inattentive, obsessed, etc.) time into live time? This is an attempt which can be made, in various manners, as a disciplined way of living . . . We can in general see and appreciate the difference between anxious calculating distracted passing of time when the present is never really inhabited or filled, and present moments which are lived attentively as truth and reality. In selfish obsessional calculation or resentment we are 'always elsewhere', and the anxiety and fear and grief which come to us all may be lived, from moment to moment, in a variety of ways as illusion or as reality.

Iris sees the way we view other people as the expression of meditative practice: 'Looking at other people is different from looking at trees or works of art . . . It matters how we see other people. Such looking is not always dialogue, indeed it is rarely mutual. Others are given to us as a spectacle which we should treat with wise respect. A loving just gaze cherishes and adds substance, a contemptuous gaze withers. A look of hatred designs to kill.'

Meditation includes art and music: 'Art is totally important – looking at pictures and listening to music and not just rushing along – it detaches you, it sets the soul into a great space and loses self – and this is not necessarily an arcane activity; it should be part of everyday life.'

She is particularly concerned that children are no longer being educated in looking at things properly. 'The visual is an image of distance and non-possession. The idea of space and quietness, thinking, seeing, attending, keeping still, not seizing, is important in all education . . . It encourages reflection, reverence and respect.

'The element of goodness, the conception of perfection can get lost in the methods of teaching. Of course it's very good that children should know science – I've seen in schools that the goal is now a kind of scientific accuracy. But the loss of literature is an aspect of the lunacy of the human soul itself. Although children should be taught to use computers and to get things right in certain ways, yet there is no effort made to see how very deep certain literature is. Throwing out Shakespeare is losing some very profound things which children ought instinctively to understand and then later on to meditate upon.'

She is not however too pessimistic about the future. She does not see 'our ordinary, fairly describable experiences of "transcendence", our apprehensions of what is good and true and real' being lost. 'A pessimistic prophecy might suggest that now, or soon, there are or will be fewer of these spiritual experiences and activities available to human beings. A nuclear war or an ecological catastrophe might blot out people and their potentialities. But if we escape such a fate, I see no reason to predict a "loss of spirit".'

Iris's love of Plato informs all her philosophical books. Plato is often accused nowadays of being the original divider of the sacred from the everyday and Platonic ideas are viewed with some antagonism by many in the New Age. But perhaps those who denounce Plato have not read him very fully. Iris, who has, finds his teachings inspirational. Plato envisaged the soul on a journey ascending through four stages of enlightenment and at each stage discovering that the reality it was living in was only a shadow or image of something more real still. At the end of its path the soul finds the Good. Then it returns. But as it moves back through the forms which previously it had only partly understood, it now sees them in their true nature and in their right relationship to each other.

'Plato's image implies that complete unity is not seen until one has reached the summit, but moral advance carries with it intuitions of unity which are increasingly less misleading ... Courage, which seemed at first to be something on its own, a sort of misplaced daring of the spirit, is now seen to be a particular operation of wisdom and love. We come to distinguish a self-assertive ferocity from the kind of courage which would enable a man coolly to choose the labour camp rather than the easy compromise with the tyrant ... Freedom, we find out, is not a case of chucking one's weight about, it is the disciplined overcoming of self. Humility is not a peculiar habit of self-effacement, rather like having an inaudible voice, it is selfless respect for reality and one of the most difficult and central of all virtues.

'There is an orientation towards goodness in the fundamental texture of human nature. We, as individuals, live in different worlds, we *see* different things, not just in general but down to last details. The Good is distant and apart, and yet it is a source of energy, it is an active principle of truthful cognition and moral understanding in the soul, the inspiration and love-object of Eros. It is not a logical universal, or a Person, it is *sui generis*. It is a "reality principle" whereby we find our way about the world. Plato's philosophy offers a *metaphysical picture* of that essential presence, together with many and various instances of our relations to it. So there is, we may say, a rainbow bridge – but no covenant . . .

'God does not and cannot exist. But what led us to conceive of him does exist and is *constantly* experienced and pictured. That is, it is real as an Idea, and is also incarnate in knowledge and work and love. This is the true idea of incarnation, and it is not something obscure. We *experience* both the reality of perfection and its distance away, and this leads us to place our idea of it outside the world of existent being as something of a different, unique and special sort. Such experience of the reality of good is not like an arbitrary and assertive resort to our own will; it is a discovery of something independent of us, where that independence is essential.

'The good man perceives the real world, a true and just seeing of people and human institutions, which is also a seeing of the invisible through the visible, the real through the apparent, the spiritual beyond the material.'

Susan Howatch

___

'Every day I would walk around the Close and I would go round and round that Cathedral. It was hypnotic – and I think I knew even then that it was going to be very special in my life.'

Susan Howatch, a rich and famous author of romantic family sagas, gave up the worldly side of her life when she found success was not making her happy. She became a recluse, simplifying her life, and went to live in the Close of Salisbury Cathedral where she experienced a powerful spiritual awakening. As she became drawn into religious life, so she was drawn into the lives of the clergy. She knew she must now write a different type of book altogether and it was here that she found a rich seam of new material. She began to write about the whole new world of Starbridge, a fictional cathedral town, based on Salisbury.

Six amazing novels were the result. They followed the lives of a group of clergymen as they clambered up the career ladder of the Church of England. The books grappled with spiritual confusion and theological crises, with sin followed by redemption, while the gripping drama and sexual intrigue of the earlier sagas was skilfully retained. In a television interview, however, Susan pointed out: 'I do *not* write knickers and vicars books. Of course sex comes into the books, but I write about human nature and human beings. I write about flawed people who attempt spiritual journeys.'

In *Glittering Images*, the first of this unusually compelling series, Susan introduces us to the way in which the masks we put on to face the world can blind us to reality. Charles Ashworth, a handsome and fashionable young clergyman, drives himself towards the verge of insanity because of his need to maintain the creation he has made of himself – the glittering image he holds in place to face the world. Because he is a strong person, he has been able to suppress for much of his life the knowledge that beneath the glittering façade there is another person altogether, unworthy and unlovable. This knowledge has not produced any cracks in his psyche until, aged thirty-seven and a widower, he is driven by his sexual needs to the point of breakdown. Jon Darrow, an Anglican monk who possesses great powers of insight, analyses the root of the breakdown. In this extract Charles speaks first:

'The problem lies in me,' my voice said. 'I'm the problem. I'm so unfit and so unworthy that I feel no woman would ever be able to cope with me.'

'And do the women you meet appear to share this view of you?'

'Oh no! But then they never meet the man I keep hidden. They just meet the man on public display.' I hesitated but added, 'I call him the glittering image because he looks so well in the mirror. But beyond him –'

'Beyond him,' said Darrow, never batting an eyelid, 'stands the angry stranger who appears in the mirror whenever the glittering image goes absent without leave.'

Charles wrestled with what that statement implied, but Darrow did not hurry him and at last he was able to utter that it must be the glittering image who wanted to get married. Is it because he wants to be seen as a model clergyman with a perfect wife, and living happily for ever, Darrow asks. Yes, says Charles, he was keen to live up to the glittering image's ideal, to find a perfect wife and live happily ever after. So you are the glittering image, suggests Darrow, and Charles agrees. All right then, replies Darrow, but what about the other Charles? What does he think of remarriage? 'He doubts that it's possible for him to marry and live happily ever after because he's so unfit and unworthy that no woman could cope with him . . .'

Jon Darrow is the 'wise man' in all the books in the series, the one person in this first book with the ability to enable Charles to penetrate to the root cause of his need for an image. In spite of his orthodox holy calling, he possesses certain unusual powers, including the power to heal.

The potent quality of *Glittering Images* is not so much the light it sheds on religion and the Church of England, as its ability to expose us to the great central problem in life – the one we all share with Charles Ashworth – the longing to be liked and admired, and the consequent need to present ourselves to the world in as admirable a way as possible:

'Charles, would I be reading too much into your remarks if I deduced that liking and approval are very important to you?'

That was an easy question to answer. 'Well, of course, they're important!' I exclaimed. 'Aren't they important to everyone? Isn't that what life's about? Success is people liking and approving of you. Failure is being rejected. Everyone knows that.'

Here Charles has stated what most people feel, but to Susan the glittering image is as much a spiritual problem as a psychological one, and at last Charles begins to understand this.

He does realize, he says, that gaining liking and approval from everyone is not the only thing worth doing in life. In fact he sees, at least intellectually, that real success is to do with following one's calling from God in as close a way as possible. He tells Darrow that he should be dedicating himself to serving God in that way – and Darrow interrupts sharply to ask 'which self?' Charles answers that it is his true self which would want to serve God like that and is suddenly struck by what he has said. Grappling with this new insight, he tells Darrow that it can only be one's true self with which one approaches God and struggles to do His will:

'Or to put it in non-theological terms,' said Darrow, allowing me time to complete the struggle, 'success involves realizing the fullest potential for good of one's true self, so that one's life is a harmonious expression of one's innate gifts. Now, Charles, how would you, your true self, define failure?'

'Locking up one's true self in order to live a lie,' said my voice. 'Living out of harmony with one's true self in order to pursue the wrong goals for the wrong reasons. Caring more about other people's opinions than about serving God and doing His will.' I added in shame, 'I can see I've been very much in error.'

Darrow is inclined to agree but points out that there is nothing intrinsically wrong with Charles's true self, which knows exactly what Charles should be doing with his life. It is the glittering image which has gained such a dominance over him that he has to spend inordinate amounts of time and energy keeping it content. As he considered this, Charles suddenly realized that it was like being blackmailed.

Darrow understands. 'Exactly. The glittering image insists that the right people won't like and approve of you unless you give him a luxurious home right in the forefront of your personality, and for some reason you're so addicted to liking and approval that you're willing to give in to this demand in order to satisfy your addiction.'

Susan has described a condition that all religions recognize – when one is fooled by one's own self-made image and is thus identified with falseness. To live continuously in such a state means that no light of reality can penetrate the wound-up toy that one has become. It is as though the true self that Charles talks about has been eclipsed by labels, as though the I is something determined from the outside, something balanced against other people and things, with only a social appearance and only a worldly evaluation; but if one thinks that *this* is the self then one has lost sight of the real self. In error one comes to assume that what is called I is a *thing* and that living from one's real self is some sort of exotic practice.

In Charles Ashworth's case the monk, Jon Darrow, helps him to track down the original cause of his split personality which is the fact, unknown to him until then, that he was not his father's child and his 'father' had been exceptionally severe with him, destroying his sense of self-worth. The analysis of his personality which leads eventually to the banishment of the glittering image does not owe anything to Freudian or Jungian analytic methods but is conducted as an essential religious task. The reader is necessarily drawn to ask herself (for the analysis is so full of insights) some profound questions as to how much of a glittering image is on show with oneself. How much of a lie is one living? How much has been acquired over the years to bolster one up and prevent people seeing how really vulnerable and lost one is?

Susan herself felt lost and vulnerable as a young woman. She was reading law but found her heart wasn't in it. And she had hoped to be a writer but novel after novel was returned. For seven years she went on getting rejection slips. Finally one such slip arrived at a time when she was also bereft of boyfriends and had come to feel a failure in both her personal and professional lives. She decided there was nothing for her in England and she would leave for America to try her luck there: 'Immediately I set foot on American soil everything went right. I met my husband and I got a book accepted for publication. That put me on the road to success.'

There was no thought of her own spiritual journey at that time. But the start of the journey is often brought about by a crisis. It is as though the true self can be glimpsed, perhaps for the first time, when we are in doubt or despair. Susan discovered this for herself.

'I had a huge financial and professional success when I was thirty [her novel *Penmarric*]. I had wanted very much to have money and fame and I got it. It was megabucks, with fast cars and champagne. It was fun at the time but something one quickly gets tired of and it didn't work out as I had expected. Success is very difficult to handle, I think. When you have the money to do anything, you have so many choices and you get confused as to which choice to make and so you probably make the wrong one. Also, it's very difficult to centre yourself. If you have to go to work, it creates a pattern. If you don't have that pattern, then you get diverted and then you feel a vacuum and try to fill it with the wrong things.

'Success had a profound effect on my marriage as it was very difficult for my husband to cope with. It was really hard for him and in the end it seemed better to separate. So my marriage broke up and I decided to leave America with my daughter. But after some time she wanted to go back to America to live with her father – she was thirteen – and when she went I felt that I was a complete failure. It turned out all right in the end because she came back after two years and now she lives just up the road. It had a happy ending, but at the time it was awful.'

Susan had tried to determine what was actually happening in her life.

'One should never seek suffering – some Christians think one should, but I'm sure one should not seek it – but if it comes to you, you must figure out what it means, make sense of it, and then it can be enlightening.

'I didn't change immediately. I became increasingly dislocated, I lost touch with reality and I was deeply perplexed and that's when I started thinking, well, maybe there is a God or maybe God really does have relevance to me.'

It was in this way that the sacred came closer to her.

'What it was, I was being stripped down and God was closing in. I

42

knew it was God because it seemed very evident that there was something out there closing in and something in here welling up. It wasn't just my conscience because my conscience was in an absolute fog and I was very disorientated. I had to assume that this thing closing in on me and shaking me until my teeth rattled was actually God. I was being shown that fame and fortune didn't make me happy, that I had been selling myself, chasing my own ends and that there was no happiness there. And the failure of my personal life was illuminated garishly in my mind and I realized that that was no good, I hadn't made myself happy there either. And out of that realization came this enormous pressure on the psyche, which I call God.

'What is God? It's a useful code word, I think, for ultimate reality, ultimate concern. Anyway, here was this great pressure and it was definitely closing in and there came a moment when it seemed so obvious that I just said, "Right. I'll stop serving myself and when I write – *if* I write – it will be for God."

'So then the next great question was did I go on writing or did God require me to do something else? That occupied me for some months. I thought I might be required to go to college and take a degree in theology and teach. So I read everything I could on Christianity and religion and took an A-level correspondence course and tried to figure out what God actually wanted. And gradually I began to make sense of it.

'And then in the end, during my reading, I came across a fascinating story and I thought There would be a wonderful novel in that! and that became *Glittering Images*. So finally I realized I was meant to go on writing but in a quite different way and my publishers were horrified.

'But now that I've finished the series it's all coming up again, so I shall think to myself what does God now require of me – because I could do all sorts of things now. Am I meant to go on writing? One has to discern what one's supposed to do and what one would be best suited to do to make the most of oneself in order to serve God properly.'

Serving God properly has become the compelling purpose of Susan's life. It is impossible, she believes, to be happy or fulfilled unless one lets this purpose motivate one's whole life.

'It's all one. Our psychological hang-ups and our spirituality, they're all related and they're all concerned with the person that one is. So if one's psyche is not aligned properly with God then one's going to lose touch with things.

'If you think of God as being like a spark in the centre of the soul, then you must line that inward spark up with the transcendent God. That's really saying you've got to be the person you were designed to be. That is the real quest for God, to get yourself lined up right. And of course you can say all this in psychological language too by saying you must be integrated, you must integrate your inner self with your ego and line it all up with the blueprint you were when you were born.

'Existence is both being and becoming – we're not here just to be, we have to become as well. So it's a journey and the more you understand yourself, the more likely it is you'll realize the person you're supposed to be. And the more that is realized, the more you will be fitting in with God's special plans for you and the happier you will be. If you're lined up properly with God, then you're much more fulfilled. But people don't realize this. They think it's all about suffering, for instance, but what it really means is effort. You have to make an effort, to sweat blood, trying to be what you're supposed to be.'

Susan's own realization had brought about *Glittering Images* and it is at the end of that particular book, when Charles has been so stripped down that he can begin to live from his real self at last, that his words reflect what his creator must also have felt when she came to that point in her own life.

'The demons departed as my mind stood open before God and once more I passed through the strait gate to set out along the narrow way in response to my mysterious call. My new life in God's service stretched before me; I knew there could be no turning back. I could only go on in the absolute faith that one day his purpose would stand fully revealed, and in the light of that faith the darkness of my anxiety was extinguished. The glittering image of the apparent world dissolved into the great truths which lay beyond and the truths were not a beautiful dream . . . but the ultimate reality. Love and forgiveness, truth and beauty, courage and compassion blazed with a radiance which far outshone the cheap glitter of illusion, and

I knew then with an even deeper conviction that in serving God man only fulfilled his need to strive to live in that eternally powerful light.'

Susan has come to accept her own conversion as a properly Christian one. 'What happened was that I found while it was going on I couldn't really talk to anyone. I felt cut off from all my friends because I thought I couldn't possibly talk about it, nobody would understand what I was going through and at that time I wasn't a churchgoer. I found it frightening and an alienating experience. I thought I was going mad. I was turned inside out. I found that all the things I had thought important were not important and all the things I had thought unimportant were vital.

'But this is a classic experience. One of the high points of my conversion was when I came across an entry in *The Dictionary of Christian Spirituality*. It describes in detail what I was going through and calls it the second journey. The second journey is when you come to the end of one phase and you go through a period of great darkness and all the markers shift. It's not uncommon with writers – Joseph Conrad went through it. When I got *The Dictionary* and found this entry listing all the symptoms, I felt, thank God! Up to then I thought I had been going nuts. When I realized it was part of quite a common syndrome, I was so relieved. It clarified things for me. I felt my first journey was behind me and I didn't want to cling to it any more. I wanted to move on into the second journey.

'I turned to Christianity, which has been going on for a long time, because I felt it was better and showed more humility to try to look for wisdom there. You can't dismiss all the wisdom in religion. You know that the best minds in all those years have been focused on it and have cut out all the dross, winnowed it down and passed it on.'

Because of her Christian path, Susan lives near Westminster Abbey. She has chosen an unpretentious flat and she keeps it bare of unnecessary furniture, so that it is possible to feel some resemblance to a nun's cell. She has decided to live a celibate life.

'I find living a solitary life is right for me. In the mystical tradition what usually happens is that people withdraw and they soak up the peace, and then they return to the fray. I did withdraw when I was living in Salisbury and I did live a very solitary life. And then gradually I've been drawn back and every time I try to escape from London, it's never any good and I always get pulled back here. So

I've given up now. I think, "Well, God wants me to be here, so that's that." And I now know more people than I did and opportunities keep springing up and I'm not quite sure what I'll make of it all. In fact there's a tremendous tension because I really like to be alone and need to be alone. In fact you have to be alone to write the sort of books that I write, to project yourself into them. I couldn't have written this series of books if I had been in a relationship. I simply would not have had the physical or mental energy to sustain a relationship with a man. At the same time it's very important to meet people and to be with people. But that tension need not be a bad thing, it can generate good ideas. So it's a problem I'm working on at the moment, how to gain the right balance, how to lead a balanced life properly – and I think that's the big challenge I have to work out for the future.'

The Abbey plays a central role in Susan's life. At the end of her conversion and when she was certain that her direction was towards Christianity, she turned towards formal religion and joined the Church of England. But she still has one or two reservations.

'I find public worship very difficult. After my religious conversion it was five years before I started going to church. That came last and I found the worship at that time very hard. I don't know why. Perhaps because I came from a non-religious family. Temperamentally I'm not good at worship. But I think there's more to worship than just trying to live properly and I now regard it as a discipline. I think that's why I bother with it. The breakthrough came for me when an old priest said, "You've got to work at worship, it's not entertainment." I realized I had been regarding it as entertainment and thinking, "Oh God, this is boring and what am I getting out of it?" and of course that's the wrong attitude. If you think of it as the spiritual equivalent of jogging or lifting weights, then I believe that's helpful. Especially if one's a mystic, the tendency is to go over the top and if you can have some disciplined framework of which worship is a part, it keeps you within rational bounds. It's not blighting one's mystical drive, it's just channelling it correctly.

'But public worship still remains hard. I've been going to church regularly now for four or five years and I still haven't mastered it. I'm better than I used to be. It's coming, but it's a long haul. I don't mind. One likes a challenge.

'I try to go to Evensong every day at the Abbey and I regard Evensong as a mantra. I know all the set pieces so well I don't even think of the words – I like it even when there's no music and it's just said. It's a mantra and you tune in. It's all a discipline and I find it very helpful to me.

'In a way, private worship is easy. Private worship is when I get up in the morning – and I don't pray in words when I'm alone – I just pull the switch in my head and tune in. But that's the mystical approach and I feel I need more than that. I need the public worship too, which I have to work at, otherwise I would be worried I would get floppy!'

Although Susan believes that God is a code word, yet she does talk about God exactly as if he were a person. But she is clear that this is not what she means.

'There is the experience of direct communication but at the same time there's acres and acres of God that we will never experience or see. God is both personal and impersonal. If you treat God personally it works, but I feel it's not a question of either personal or impersonal but of both. I believe God is transcendent and immanent. By which I mean that if I'm a writer I'm outside my creation, sitting at my typewriter, and at the same time I'm inside my creation because I'm in every word, in all of the characters. So I'm transcendent outside and immanent inside.

'But you must have a word – a code word – for this ultimate mystery, this ultimate concern, and I think God is very suitable because it ties in with the whole realm of human experience. But it still remains a mystery, a journey into infinity, and you never get to the bottom of it – not in this life, anyway. The spiritual journey never stops, it goes on to the grave and then, we assume, goes on beyond. The thing is, we're so limited in our understanding. We all are. So when people say "I don't believe in God", very often what they're saying is "I don't believe in an old man with curly white whiskers up in a cloud" or in some other sort of simple image. But God can't be confined to images. So although I use the word God as a useful code word, I know that the reality of God can't be encompassed by any word.

'Christ is a code word too and I don't see how people can do without Christ. If you think of the Trinity as an arrangement –

47

mathematical, if you like – which reflects reality, you can see that God is the idea and Christ is the way the idea is expressed, that which makes it intelligible to human beings. The Holy Spirit is the actual way the idea is assimilated by us. So God and Christ form a twin aspect of reality.

'You have God. He's got to work in some way that we can't understand. So the point about Jesus Christ is that he enacted in flesh and blood the ultimate truth. He presented these truths in a way which human beings can grasp more easily. From the point of view of concepts I do think the Trinity is a useful device for actually grappling with these difficult things.'

Susan has explained the Church's doctrine of the Trinity and from that point of view no doubt she is right. But is it really necessary to 'grapple with these difficult things'? To all non-Christian readers of this chapter there must be a temptation to say: forget the concepts, Susan. The Trinity was largely conceived as a doctrine and its finer points worked out at the fourth-century Council of Constantinople and it has often caused more confusion than clarity. Although it may be a way of tying up the concepts of God, Christ and Spirit, perhaps it would be better, even for a Christian, not to create yet more concepts as explanations of the first.

But Susan also presents another version of Christ, one for which she feels perhaps more deeply than for the mathematical equation.

'The point about Christ is he was God-centred, perfectly integrated. He didn't think of himself; he was lined up correctly with God. He was the most human human it's possible to have, perfectly integrated. The more human we are, the more we become like God, the more we become divine. So Christ, being wholly human, was also wholly divine.'

Again, Susan may leave her non-Christian reader behind here. But from the way her novels are targeted to reveal the split between who you think you are and who you really are, we can see that for her there is an ideal of a delusion-free person (just as Iris Murdoch's ideal was the selfless person), one who has dropped all the armour of the glittering image and lives entirely from the true self, the true human beneath the delusion, and who is thus totally aligned with what Susan calls God, and Taoists might call the Way.

There is no doubt at all that many people lose sight of the reality of themselves and consequently experience much pain and suffering. They lose sight of the life of the true self, believing themselves to be determined all the time by outside events and circumstances and feeling they can only respond by adopting one role or another: putting on the clothes of family or class or status or wealth. And although these are just the clothes we wear between naked birth and naked death, most people are taken in by them and never ask what is the naked self. But for some there comes a moment, as it did for Susan, when they feel a hollowness in their lives and begin to see through the clothes to the naked self and from then on they can never again quite believe in the clothes.

Are religious ideas clothes, in the same way that status and fame are? In spite of her Christian beliefs Susan is open to the understanding that at least some religious ideas might be – even Christ: 'The power of the Spirit, I think that's more helpful than Christ somehow. One can see the effect it has and what it draws out of people.'

Perhaps there are more of us who can accept the power of the Spirit than can accept the Trinity. But the power of the Spirit too, if defined too conceptually, becomes an idea rather than an experience; and once it is in the realm of ideas it can be anybody's tool, as is shown in the myriad religious wars which have plagued humanity.

How do hatred and war come about? Are there powerful dark forces, as well as light?

'I do believe in dark forces. We perceive them with our minds and I think evil is a force. But evil may be a way of projecting outwards some very difficult components of the human mind. Perhaps we are giving these components objective reality by talking of them as forces. And it may just be a question of language. After all, ghosts. You can think of a ghost as an objective reality which is not normally available to your conscious mind; or you can think of it as not an objective reality at all but a projection from your unconscious mind. But in both cases you are talking about something which is not usually available to consciousness and that's how these dark forces work, whether they're internal or external.

'There's a theory that evil is the absence of good, but I don't think that's sufficient to account for it. If you've ever seen evil eyeball to eyeball, then you know it exists. I explain it by the theory that the world is still being created – God is still creating the world – and in any act of creation there is always mess and you make mistakes. You can't create without having these dark areas. But the whole point is that at the end of the creative process every step is redeemed. I tend to think of it like my work. I make mistakes and tear a lot up but when I hold the completed book in my hand I know that I couldn't have reached that point without all my mess and all my mistakes. I had to go through the dark side and the errors in order to get the whole thing right. So I think evil is some sort of side-effect of the creative process. It's something that shouldn't exist and eventually will be ironed out. But it's probably required in order for the process to get where it's going to go.

'But God is always going to be in there, redeeming. It's rather like connecting the garden hose to the tap. If you connect it properly, the water's going to flow better. If you line yourself up properly, the power of redemption has a better chance of flowing through. But if it's not hooked up right, you're going to get a lot of spillage and wastage.'

Whatever scepticism readers might feel about the possibility that God is still creating the world and making some mistakes on the way, we should remember that from the point of view of science the big bang is not yet over. When that explosion first happened, billions of years ago, the conscious world was created, and consciousness has not come to a standstill any more than has the evolving universe. So whatever we feel about God and his actions, the theory itself in different language seems to be correct. And evil might well be one of the manifestations of the branch on the evolutionary tree that is us at this particular time.

Susan herself is fascinated by natural science and its relationship to religion. She has endowed a lectureship at Cambridge with a million pounds to study theology and natural science. She has linked the two because she feels that traditionally they have been far apart and now need to come together.

'In the twentieth century we've sat around in our little disciplines and people haven't communicated their wisdom to each other. I think in the twenty-first century there's going to be much more in the way of interdisciplinary studies. The more we pool our knowledge the wider it will be. Science and religion don't actually tackle the same things, but they should be complementary and not opposed. Religion gives the meaning and the value, and science describes the world about us. They don't tackle the same aspects of truth and the most helpful thing for most disciplines would be if there was more interchange between them. In the nineteenth century religion was very scathing about science and pooh-poohed the whole thing in a thoroughly haughty way. In the twentieth century it's all been reversed and science has become very grand and done the same thing to religion. So in the twenty-first century I think it's time for both disciplines to show humility and to learn from each other. They've both got so much to learn. Some of the scientists think they're an élite who know the truth and nothing must be allowed to impinge on it. But I think that attitude is not in the best interests of scientific research.

'So the idea of a lectureship where both theology and natural science can co-exist is sending out a message, which is that both disciplines need to be taken seriously and must be put into perspective and into relationship with each other. I think science can shed a great light on Christianity and I'm sure it will be the future, it will be the next development. The world is God's world. All these things must eventually link up.

'Religion, after all, is powered by the language of symbols – metaphors and analogies – and science too is powered by the language of symbols but not the same ones, its symbols are mathematical. So however we approach the truth we're going to use metaphors and symbols because we're so limited and that's the only way we can get at it. But there are different symbols and we need to understand them and mesh them together. I feel there's a lot of hard academic work to be done and it must be done on the highest level or it's not worth anything. So that's really the basis of this lectureship.'

In the books which followed *Glittering Images* Susan explored the paranormal, perhaps as part of her interest in natural science and the mysterious powers of the mind. Supernatural events and their consequences are particularly present in the penultimate book of the series, *Mystical Paths*. Here the action revolves around Nicholas Darrow, the now aged Jon Darrow's quite young son (Jon had left the monastery and married in late middle age). Nicholas, who believes himself to be exactly like his father, is training to be a priest. He is also sure he is a psychic and capable of the unusual powers his father possesses. He is arrogantly certain of his own opinions. One of his reasons for his career is the image he has of Jesus as a sure winner, on whose side he wants to be – 'I had wanted to be a priest ever since I learnt in my early childhood about Jesus the healer and the exorcist, the hero who always triumphed over the dark.'

The book follows his many ghastly mistakes with the paranormal. One, in particular, dictates the course of the book. A friend, Christian, has disappeared and is assumed dead. His widow, Katie, is distraught and is brought to Nicholas by another friend, Marina, so that he can hypnotize Katie into a better frame of mind. The hypnosis is easy; she is an excellent subject. But when he says the Lord's Prayer to bring her out of the hypnosis, and reaches the words 'deliver us from evil', a picture crashes to the ground and Katie gives a chilling non-human sound. Marina screams and Nicholas finds he cannot bring Katie back to consciousness. At last he gets her to open her eyes, but in the meantime his attention has wandered and been caught by the fallen picture. The glass is still intact, which seems miraculous.

He tries to get the girls to pray with him but they are too distracted and so is he. 'Then the inevitable happened. I suddenly became aware of a discarnate shred elbowing its way into our circle . . . I experienced the shred as a strong sinister pressure on the psyche.

'Automatically I said, "Lord Jesus Christ, Son of God, have mercy on me, a sinner."'

Nicholas felt the pressure ease but by this time his psychic grip on Katie had diminished and she was moaning in an eerie way. He felt the whole situation was impossible, because he had to control the shred and Katie, and Marina, who was now about to panic. Then the table started to rock and Marina screamed.

Nicholas was highly alarmed but instantly called on Jesus and tried to reassure Marina at the same time. Things began to calm down. He put the table back on its four legs and felt he should calm himself as much as possible. It must all be due to Katie letting off a 'gale-force blast of energy', he decided. It was no more than that and no reason to feel panic. He persuaded himself it was all just an inconvenience and it seemed very odd to him that he could not imprint PEACE and LOVE on Katie's mind. He could not understand why he now found he could not make contact with her any more, and he wondered if, during the table chaos, the sinister discarnate shred which he had expelled from his own mind had entered hers and was barring her psyche against him. Then, suddenly, he realized that the shred was closing in on him to attack him again:

I could feel the pressure mounting, I could feel the power behind the pressure, and the next moment I knew that beyond the power, blasting it forward, was –

I leapt to my feet, my chair flew backwards and simultaneously the glass shattered to pieces in the frame of the fallen engraving. I had a fleeting glimpse of Marina's terrified face, and then I slammed my psyche shut against the Dark by a colossal act of will. I heard myself shout out: 'IN THE NAME OF JESUS CHRIST, BE GONE FROM THIS ROOM!'

The curtains billowed violently by the open window and Katie slumped forward across the table in a dead faint.

In this excerpt, and indeed in much of the rest of the book, Susan opens up the occult world to us and implies the existence of 'discarnate shreds', Satan, and the like. It is a world which certainly seems to be the preoccupation of many Christians, particularly in the Church of England which takes it very seriously and where there's at least one exorcist attached to every diocese. But Susan ensures that her readers are not tied down by supernatural explanations only and gives us a psychological interpretation as well. When Nicholas recounts the episode to his father, Jon Darrow takes it to pieces:

'I should think it most unlikely that the Devil could have been bothered to drop in on your shoddy little seance. It's much more probable that you lost your nerve and began to fantasize once the energy disturbances spiralled out of control. I assume there were energy disturbances?'

'Yes, and Katie was in a sort of coma, moaning and groaning as if she were possessed –'

'Rubbish, of course she wasn't possessed! She was merely manifesting her deep psychological troubles . . .'

'But, father, that force I experienced – okay, maybe it wasn't the devil himself, maybe it was just a malign shred acting alone – well, whatever it was, it came from without. It wasn't welling up from within.'

'How did you experience it?'

'As a mounting pressure on the psyche.'

'Exactly. It was a pressure exerted by your unconscious mind – which in your manic state would have seemed quite external to your ego.'

'But father –'

'All right, Nicholas, calm down. I think our disagreement is an illusion created by the fact that we're mixing up two different languages, the religious language employing symbols such as "the Devil" and the scientific language which employs concepts such as "the unconscious mind". Why don't we produce a version of your story in each language so that we can see we're talking about a single truth.'

Jon Darrow then proceeds to point out that whatever language they use, unpleasant forces had been there in the room. Katie was in a highly disturbed state and Nicholas too was disturbed when he could no longer keep control. In religious terminology Katie was infested by a demon, the demon of guilt (she felt she had failed in her marriage), and when Nicholas realized this his psyche had opened up to Katie so that the demon was tempted to leave Katie and go to Nicholas. Nicholas then repelled the demonic invasion by calling on Christ and aligning himself with Christ's power.

But the psychological way of explanation was to use other symbols, ones which would not diminish the religious experience but complement and confirm it. Katie's demonic infestation could be seen as a neurosis – that she was obsessed with a sense of guilt, rooted in her unconscious but now breaking through into her conscious mind. Under hypnosis her normal control left her, with the result that chaotic emotions began to arise and manifest themselves in frightening forms.

She might or might not have been undergoing a psychotic phase but her behaviour had had the same terrifying effect on Nicholas as if he were watching a schizophrenic. This terror had combined with his own guilt at having brought the situation about. It all came to seem like a highly dangerous invasive force and in an instinctive gesture of begging for help, he had invoked the name of Christ 'which is the point where our two languages meet. The invocation gave you the confidence to regain control, or in other words, the invocation resulted in an outpouring of grace which enabled you to triumph over evil,' concludes Jon Darrow.

This clever device of bringing in the language of psychology to explain the language of the Bible is one which Susan uses throughout her books and it is what makes them relevant to a modern reader. But she herself has never had the supernatural experiences of her characters although she researches them very carefully and only uses those which are well-known phenomena. Does she believe in the supernatural? In her reasonable way, she says yes.

'I do believe in it. But one has to be very careful about dealing with the paranormal and draw a distinction between it and religious mysticism. They overlap to a certain extent but the best mystics have always said that paranormal phenomena can attend mystical experience but are a distraction. On the spiritual path you might bump into the paranormal but really it has nothing to do with anything else, it's just a sort of reflex. On the other hand, there's no doubt that some mystical experience does have a paranormal aspect, so you have to be very careful. I'm interested in the paranormal but I try to approach it very rationally and sceptically. There are rational explanations for most peculiar things but not for all. There are things without explanation.

'What we're really dealing with is the mystery of consciousness. We communicate with God through consciousness and God speaks to us through consciousness and we communicate with each other through consciousness – and sometimes consciousness has this strange dimension.

'If you think of it as a stream, then we're all interlinked by consciousness and probably when human beings were less developed we relied on the paranormal dimension more than we do now.

'We don't understand how consciousness operates. The evidence of extra-sensory perception is overwhelming and also for clairvoyance – for seeing the future. So you've got to account for that and it's no good closing your mind to it and believing that it doesn't happen. But one must approach it very cautiously. We can only be agnostic about what happens after death, for instance, because we simply don't know. But, having said that, the near-death experience is extremely interesting.'

The mystery of death is by no means ignored in Susan's books and exorcism is one of the themes in *Mystical Paths*. A priest, Lewis, exorcizes a chapel. Nicholas, who was present, asks what really goes on in an exorcism. Is it that the exorcist sets tormented souls at rest and expels the pollution they have caused? Or is it that he sets free the still living by casting out the shadows the dead have left on their subconscious minds?

Lewis replies that it is not a question of either/or because if it is simplified too much the understanding of a complex situation is lost. Nicholas asks:

'So you really believe that exorcism affects both the living and the dead?'

'Yes, but of course we can't see directly the effect on the dead. That's something which can only be psychically intuited, but what we do see, often very clearly, is the effect of the exorcism on the living who have been reflecting the dead person's torment . . .'

All through her books Susan digs into these difficult questions and presents answers in the languages of religion, science and psychology. From her own account of herself we know she feels that this is what God intended her to do. It is appropriate to end with the thoughts she puts into Nicholas's mind, but which indeed originate in her own.

And now once more I see with my psychic eye the Holy Spirit moving across the dark waters of the earth in a ceaseless outpouring of light and air . . . And as I see far beyond time and space to the mystery that veils the Godhead, I can feel at the centre of my being the spark which connects me to that ultimate mystery, the mystery which no man will ever unfold this side of the grave. All one can do in this life is to embark on that journey to the centre, where the immanent God dwells, and fight to continue that journey no matter how many obstacles are thrust in one's path. I know that to serve the mysterious transcendent God to the best of my ability I must continually work to align myself with the immanent God, the God within. I must continually strive to realize the blueprint of my personality and become the man God created me to be.

Danah Zohar

'Most writers, and indeed most physicists, find it impossible to discuss the sub-atomic processes outlined by quantum theory without falling back on adjectives like bizarre, weird, erratic and magical to describe the ghostly particles and interactions which lie just beneath the surface of our day-to-day world.'

Danah Zohar was thirteen when she first encountered a new world, the world of the atom. In Toledo, Ohio – her birthplace – she had been taken shopping by her mother to buy a present for a boy whose birthday party she was going to and on the way back they stopped at the laundromat to do some washing. 'There was nothing else to do so I sat reading this boy's present, a book about the atom. And it was just wildly exciting. I had never read such interesting things.'

It was in this way that her life-long commitment to discovering the nature of reality in all its aspects began. 'I got very excited about the atom and I had the good luck to have an imaginative science teacher that year and he gave me other books about it. I was a passionate sort of child and once I had found something that interested me I became excessively involved with it, so it was the atom from then on. I got to quantum physics by about the age of sixteen, just by reading books and teaching myself and asking questions of teachers. I was able to read David Bohm's book on quantum physics at that time and then somehow the questions that teenagers ask – well, I had asked them since I was five, I suppose – who am I, what am I doing here and what's going to happen to me when I die – somehow quantum physics seemed to speak to all these questions. The answers might not have stood up in a laboratory very well but they spoke to the mixture of poetry and science that passed for quantum physics in my teenage mind. The physics seemed to help me answer all the large questions about the meaning of life and the nature of the universe and where I might fit into the scheme of things. It gave me the impression that the universe was alive and there was all this activity and creativity out there. This replaced the bleak vision that perhaps comes to all of us just through our culture, through mainstream science, of a dead and silent universe, a clockwork one where we don't find ourselves reflected in it anywhere. By contrast, in the quantum world, somehow my teenage self seemed to feel "Here I am!"'

During those teenage years and with the occasional donation of money from her grandmother, Danah transformed her bedroom into a laboratory where she built a cloud chamber, essential for tracking atoms. 'But when I brought the glass cylinder with its bits and pieces of metal attachments into the bedroom, my stepfather got suspicious. I needed large quantities of methyl alcohol to activate the chamber, and as this hit the dry ice in the coolant box, billowing gusts of smelly steam hit the air.' Her mother came on the scene but she was able to persuade her that the work wasn't going to blow them all up and she was allowed to go on with it. But when she added an accelerator powered by a generator and made long sparks like lightning bolts jump off the stainless steel to frighten her younger sisters, her stepfather put his foot down: '"Damn it, Lily, I'm not going to lie there in my own bed at night and be sterilized by that ray gun of hers," he shouted at Mother. "She's got to be stopped."'

Danah's mother was so confused by it all that she allowed him to call the local Civil Defence investigating team, who moved the equipment out to the garage, made Danah wear a lead apron when she was running the accelerator, and forbade her to use it at night because it was affecting the local television. But despite the restrictions, she persevered and at the end of four years was chosen to exhibit her equipment at the Seattle World's Fair. She was competing against nearly four hundred other contestants but she won the first prize for physics and a place at the world-renowned Massachusetts Institute of Technology. Her career was assured, or so it seemed, and Mrs Nixon, the wife of the President, wrote to congratulate her.

But then she entered her years of rebellion. 'When I got to MIT it was like having a bucket of cold water thrown in my face. MIT was so reductionist and Newtonian, I just hated it and during all my four years there I rebelled every inch of the way, wailing against technology.' When she had taken her degree, she gave it up, all science, and went off to Harvard to do a doctorate in philosophy and religion.

And now her rebellion against the simple Christianity of her childhood was also taking form. In her early years she had lived with her grandparents in rural Ohio and had imbibed a 'very traditional old-style Methodism believing absolutely in Jesus and the hereafter'. Later, when she had gone to live with her mother in the city, the more diluted Methodism she encountered did not appeal to her and eventually she joined the Unitarians, who seemed to have a wider outlook. She stayed with the Unitarians while she was at MIT but started to feel that there was a certain rootlessness about them. She began to be attracted to Judaism: 'At MIT at least half the student body was Jewish and so were many professors. They seemed to have a sense of rootedness about them and since my childhood had been spent with the Old Testament and my Unitarian years had emphasized the Jewish roots of the New Testament, I felt myself very close to the Jews. Their community sense and their identity was firmly rooted and this, as a rootless American, appealed to me.'

And then she discovered the Holocaust. 'I was twenty-one and I knew nothing about it. It had never been mentioned in my school years at all, no hint of it. What happened was that I overheard a professor I greatly admired advising another professor to read Elie Wiesel's novel, *Night*, which is about Auschwitz. Since I would read anything this professor recommended, I rushed out and bought *Night*. It affected me so strongly – I sat reading it in the deserted university buildings at Christmas – that I had to fly home.

'I was overwhelmed with a sense of guilt that the people to whom I belonged, the Christians, had done this to the people I now went to college with and whom I liked so much. I felt that Christians had to atone and that they could best atone by replacing some of those Jews that had been murdered. I began to study Judaism and it made sense to me in a way that Christianity no longer did.

'And so I made an Orthodox conversion when I was a student at Harvard. I took a Jewish name, the name I still use, and went off to live in Israel.'

But Israeli life was not altogether what Danah had expected and to her surprise she found herself missing the rigour of the teaching at Harvard. So she returned and finished her doctorate. And she still thought no more about science. It was not until years later when she married Ian Marshall, an English psychiatrist who was studying a quantum theory of the mind, that she was reminded of it. But even then it was to reject it.

'I very usefully said to him for about five years, why are you wasting your time on this? Who cares whether there's quantum physics in the brain or not? To which he would always reply, "It's important."

'Then I went to hospital to have an operation. I had taken material with me for a book I hoped to write. I came out of the anaesthetic and, like a vision, the book that I had never thought of writing, *The Quantum Self*, was in my head. I hadn't planned it or thought about it but when I woke up, there it was, the whole book was there. I asked the nurses to prop me up in bed and for about sixteen hours nonstop I wrote the outline of *The Quantum Self*. And I suddenly saw that what Ian was doing with quantum physics in the brain *was* tremendously important and had huge implications about the nature of the self and identity, and our relationship to the universe and everything else.'

The Quantum Self took some time to complete. Although the outline was there, it needed a lot of work to add flesh to the bones and Danah's energy and time were taken up by her two young children. But eventually it was published to considerable acclaim. Danah and her husband have collaborated on the book which followed it, *The Quantum Society*, and several more are planned, including *The Quantum Spirit*.

As our millennium draws to a close it seems as though new ways of thinking about ourselves and the universe are making themselves felt. From the distant perspective of space, for instance – which we are now able to know about – most of the wars and quarrels of the world appear as nonsensical as children's nursery fights. It is the oneness of the human race, clinging to its precarious but exquisitely beautiful globe of rock and matter in a vast void, that shakes the mind. Then, too, communications which now use electronic highways all around the planet to carry words, pictures, music and mathematics almost instantly are changing our perceptions, perhaps as significantly as when it was discovered the earth was round and revolved around the sun. Medical researchers have discovered that DNA is essential for life not only in humans, but in animal and plant forms as well. DNA makes all life one.

Humanity, for its own sake, must begin to think and to live differently and more in accord with the new knowledge that can be so

liberating. Danah sees quan...
only to the intellect but to ...
implications.

In recent years more and more ...
new world view is emerging and tha...
the key to the unfolding of a more holist...
looking at ourselves and our relationship...
been a surge of books and articles linking...
holism, with Eastern mysticism, with healing, ...
ena and much else. There have been groping ... press
something that is 'in the air', the longing for unity ... desire to
find a unifying explanation for our existence. In the a... for instance,
Annie Dillard has written a book exploring the effect of the new
physics on the fiction of this century. She has called it *Living by
Fiction*, to express the knowledge that we can never know reality as it
truly is because the very fact of observing it changes it. Tom Stopp-
ard's play, *Arcadia*, explores time and how it does not exist in the way
we think it does, so that past and present worlds can, and even
probably do, exist together.

The very term quantum physics, though, is enough for most
people at once to feel a sense of confused blankness in the mind. But
Danah is reassuring: 'I don't think that to follow the quantum vision
about spirituality or politics or anything else, one has to understand
the mathematics of quantum physics.'

If we want to change society, she says, we must start by radically
changing the way we think. Mere surface changes are not enough for
a deep social transformation. Proper transformation demands that
we change our *categories* of thinking, that we alter the basic mind
framework within which we interpret all our experiences and perceptions. We must learn a new language and this is where the quantum
vision begins.

She believes that our present social perceptions and attitudes – all
the ways in which we think about ourselves and others and the
natural world – reflect 'a long immersion' in mechanistic thought
and values. Such mechanistic ways of thinking include what we believe about material substance, about identity, about space and time
and movement, and about relationship and causality. These are the
categories that we inhabit every day as we go about our lives. We've

...ys of thinking that they seem natural. And ...uggestion that there might be some other, some ...nt, way to perceive reality, we feel at a loss, perhaps ...raged. In the physical sciences, quantum physics has caused ...t outrage.'

This is because quantum physics has discovered strange and bizarre facts about what we consider 'reality' and they are facts that are very hard even for scientists to accept, let alone the rest of the world. Danah believes that if we could learn to look at these facts it would transform much of our everyday thinking. The problem is not so much with quantum reality as with what we believe is our own common sense – our conditioned mechanistic responses. She quotes the Nobel physicist Richard Feynman, who said: 'The paradox is only a conflict between reality and your feeling of what reality ought to be.'

Danah points out that the 'new' physics is in fact nearly seventy years old and is the most successful physical theory ever. It has given us nuclear power, laser beams and the micro-chip. Yet the details of quantum physics and the immense revolution of thinking that underlies it have made no impact on the way we see ourselves or the world around us because we just don't understand it. Our minds just don't work in that way.

'When quantum physicists tell us that there is no distance between objects, or indeed no solid objects in the sense that we mean them, and that the whole notion of "separate" has no basis in reality, we are at a loss. When they ask us to give up our common-sense notions of time and tell us that "causation" is not the only way for things to be connected, we are left not knowing how to structure the events and relationships around us. We are left with a choice between crying "That's impossible!" and the realization that we must learn to see the world around us in a new way.'

'It makes me so happy,' says Valentine in *Arcadia*, 'to be at the beginning again, knowing almost nothing. A door like this has cracked open five or six times since we got up on our hind legs. It's the best possible time to be alive, when almost everything you knew is wrong.'

Danah's purpose in all her work is to make that crack in the door, that new way of seeing – which she feels is essentially a religious way

– more natural to us so that our 'exhausted and needlessly narrow habits of thought' can be revitalized and inspired by entirely new concepts.

'We are looking for some new way to be close to the source of things – whether you want to call that source God or Being or the Void. We want this new religious vision to be one that can somehow see human beings as part of the world around us – not as something separate or in some way up on a pedestal. Not as masters of the universe but as servants of the universe.

'The question is, how do we find this new vision of religion? What's the best way into it, the best way to understand it and to practise it? This is a time when people have a great religious sense, perhaps a stronger one than there has been for some time, but it's in the form of a yearning more than a fulfilment at this stage. We don't know how to incarnate this new religious feeling.

'The old western religious paradigm was very much one of belief. We were told that certain things from revelation or tradition were the truth and you practised religion by believing those things. It's the western way to work things out with the mind and say "now this is what we should believe". Science goes about things in a different way. Science approaches things through understanding, through a knowledge of how things work and what they are. Then, there's the more mystical path, which is one of experience and direct relationship to whatever it is that's at the source of things. I would like to try to bring together the latter two – understanding and experience. I think the belief paradigm is perhaps outdated by now.

'Any religious system or experience is based on asking searching questions – who are we, what are we doing here, what is the purpose of our being here and what is our relation to all else that is – what is our place in the scheme of things? All the great religions are trying in some sense to answer this. It is also the case that science is trying to answer these same questions. The scientist is also saying, what is human nature, why are human beings here and how did we get here? Scientists don't ask so much why as how and what questions. But I want to put all these questions together and try to get them into dialogue. If my work is about anything it's about trying to get scientific knowledge in dialogue with our own direct experience as human and spiritual beings. I think this is where the real richness for the future lies – in this dialogue between science and our actual intuition and experience of being human.

'The most distinctive thing about the whole western tradition up until the last few years has been dualism. Dualism has stamped its mode on the whole western experience. It began with the Greeks, with Socrates. In many of his dialogues Socrates makes the distinction between the world of experience and the world of ideas. When Socrates takes hemlock he rejoices that he will be rid of his body which so distracted him and will be able to concentrate on what really matters. So there's this tremendous split in Greek thought between the wonderful world of ideas and the cave down here where we all live.

'This same split was taken up into mainstream Christianity, so we have St Paul's talk of "rid me of this vile body of death" and it has made a terrible tradition. It sees the physical world as burdensome at least and bad at most. And it goes together with the Old Testament view that God created the world for us. So although we were here from the beginning and are part of evolution, we apparently come along after the party's over and take charge of everything and it's all for us, we are now the masters. Masters of a world of which we are not fully part because we are made of some different substance – our immortal souls are created in the image of this God who is himself not in any way physical. All the things that make us human – our creativity, our spirituality and our intelligence – are mental things which we get directly from God and the physical world is just a kind of thing that is there. So this terrible dualism comes right on up the ages. It had a kind of philosophical blessing in the seventeenth century when Descartes made the most cogent split between mind and body by saying "I know that I am a mind and I know that I have a body but the two are not the same."

'Now this split got absolutely put on a pedestal with Newtonian physics and that's where my story really begins. The main inheritance, that main bedrock of the world view that we live with today, is coming from Newtonian or classical physics. Newton took this mind–body split and said, let's concentrate on the body aspect and see what's specific to the physical world. This was the beginning of science as we know it and indeed it was a necessary step then, because to the extent that there was any science at all in medieval times it was all bound up with psychic influences and alchemy, and the world was thought to be held in place by the power of the angels. So Newton said let's clear ourselves of all the psychic influences and just concentrate on the physical and see what we can say about it.

'And he arrived at his famous three laws of motion. He discovered that if you just concentrate on this physical world it's very law-abiding. You can predict things from it, you can measure it, you can learn a great deal about it and you can use it and manipulate it.

'Newton's physics were atomistic. The world consisted of separate pieces of physical reality, each located in its own isolated space and place in time. And he conceived of these atoms as being like billiard balls and when two of these balls hit each other all they could do was bounce off each other and go their separate ways. It became in politics a model for conflict and confrontation in society.

'The second feature is that it's deterministic. Things happen because they have to happen. For Newton, God made a plan, wound up the universe and let it run on for ever afterwards. He showed that B will always follow A in exactly the same way as the forces acting on A. And you can predict this without any error.

'This was an enormous breakthrough because people had lived in an uncertain world, victims of strange storms and odd physical events, and they felt like helpless pawns in the face of such conditions. And then the scientists come along and say that this physical world is predictable and therefore controllable.

'The third characteristic of the Newtonian world was reductionist. The way a scientist in a Newtonian spirit studies things is to take any whole and break it down into its separate parts, to analyse these parts and to say the whole works the way it does because the parts have certain properties. So, if you take human beings in this reductionist way, you think, well, we are hearts and lungs and kidneys and brains – what makes us human is the way these work.

'And fourthly Newtonian physics made a tremendous split between subjects and objects, between observers and observed, between the scientist and what the scientist studies. The world of mind, of expectation, of hopes and dreams, has no part to play in the scientist's study. He's supposed to look objectively and coldly at the data and study them in that spirit and this is an important part of scientific method.

'All this had tremendous implications for a culture that looked to physics as the most powerful example of new thinking in its time. Science is always bound up with the culture of the times. You can look at what scientists are saying and see what all of us are beginning to think. Newtonian science was bound up with the Protestant Reformation, with the rise of industrialism and with the rise of rationalism. Atomism was very linked to individualism and the subject–object split became important in an anti-ecological attitude, for science could say that it could control the environment, that nature is there for us to use for our ends – and that got caught up in the Christian Biblical attitude of having dominion over nature. Then the technologist comes along and says, not only do I give you dominion but I also give you the tools to do the job. So the world becomes object and we subjects make it so.

'Many of us have a model in our minds, coming up from the old world of Newton, about who we are. We're supposed to be mind-machines, radically different from the rest of the world and standing outside it. We either have no role to play in this world, which is the depressed view: we're aliens arrived in a world we don't know. Or we're king of evolution, the master; our task to mould the world to our own ends. But in no way in this Newtonian view are we part of the world.'

Danah thinks it would be right for us to turn to quantum physics to say who we are. 'After all, there is only one reality and we're all part of it. In my view, God, or Being, or the Source – whatever you want to call it – is part of the same thing that you and I are part of. There's the one thing here. And physics is, if you like, the tool that God uses to work in this world. So I believe quite strongly that each thing that is has a physics. And in some important way our consciousness is clearly related to the structure . . . of our brains. And the potentiality of the brain is in turn somehow related to the physics of the brain.'

Danah explains in simple ways some of the quantum discoveries that most of us never hear about. For instance, bosons. Bosons are 'particles of relationship', nuclear, magnetic and gravitational. 'They are the most primary antecedents of consciousness but they also bind together the material world.' The fundamental building blocks of that material world are fermions (for example, electrons and protons) which 'tend to be anti-social and prefer to keep themselves to themselves'. Without bosons fermions would rarely come together and build anything, but without fermions bosons would have nothing to draw into relationship. So from the very beginning, from the most primary level of what is now our extraordinary world of consciousness, those building blocks of matter which are the fermions and the mysterious building blocks of consciousness which are the bosons, were necessarily interlocked in a creative dialogue.

In a far more complex form we later evolved as part and parcel of the basic yet amazing dynamic through which the universe itself unfolds. When we understand the origins of consciousness – that it exists wherever two bosons come into contact – it might not be too wild to speculate, Danah suggests, that the evolution of consciousness itself is the steady force that lies behind that unfolding. Some people might call this Mind creating the world, but Danah cannot go as far as that. For her it is more that the elementary building blocks of Mind (bosons) were there at the start of creation and were the essential partners in that creation. Through the necessary act of fulfilling their nature as 'relationship' they call forth the conscious world. Without the bosons there could not be the universe as we know it. Danah calls bosons the 'glue' which holds things together. At the same time, though, without such complex creatures as ourselves, the way in which the universe unfolds might have been slower and more limited. As consciousness increases, so the unfolding seems to speed up.

There are four other things that it's good to know about physics, Danah tells us. 'The first is that whereas the old physics was atomistic – analysing everything into its separate parts and atoms – the new physics is holistic. In quantum physics there's no such thing as separateness. All things consist of particles and waves and while the particles stay somewhat separate, the waves overlap and combine and get entangled, as the physicists say. So the physicist is telling us that we live in an entangled universe. In some sense the space that seems to be between us and everything else is an illusion. Each of us has a particle aspect – which is what we're aware of – which has a kind of boundary to it. And we also have a wave aspect that's literally extending across the universe. So my influence and your influence extends everywhere and in so doing is entangled with everything else in the universe. We live in a world that is totally interconnected.

'But there is also the particle aspect that does stay separate. But the particle has a shifting, flexible, ever-changing boundary, changing all the time in dialogue with its environment, and never staying hard like a Newtonian atom. There are no hard and fast boundaries in quantum physics between us and things – such as between me and a table or a speck of dust – even in the particle aspect. We're all entangled. And with the wave aspect we're radically entangled.

'The wave aspect is our potentiality. It's our "what might be". The particle aspect is what is, our actuality. So our potentiality to become whatever we're becoming is entangled with the potentiality to become of all else in the universe.

'Quantum physics is also radically indeterminate. In the old physics something happened because it had to happen and it was predictable. But in the new, you can't predict anything. Any single quantum event is wholly unpredictable – we don't quite know where it's coming from, nor where it's going to nor how it will get there.'

This is the uncertainty principle. In theory it is possible for anything to happen. Electrons, which circle an atomic nucleus in the way that planets circle the sun, can change their pattern when they are disturbed and then they have an unlimited number of new energy states available to them – unlimited free will. But the strange thing is that this wide-open possibility very quickly gives way to probability and the electron will in fact head for the most comfortable option – which is the state in which it will have to put out least energy to carry on travelling round the nucleus. 'Thus the electron's theoretically unlimited freedom of choice is in fact greatly restricted by laziness!' Danah adds.

She takes the example of a coffee cup to show this distinction between the possible and the probable. The uncertainty principle implies that it is perfectly possible for a coffee cup to lift itself up, float across the room and settle down somewhere else. But because of the enormous energy required for such a feat it is highly unlikely that it will ever do so. It is totally improbable. Wryly, Danah draws the analogy with ourselves. We too behave in predictable and conditioned ways. 'With rare exceptions human beings, in company with electrons, very seldom exercise the right to choose freely from among the wide range of possibilities held open to them by God or the uncertainty principle.'

The old Newtonian world had no concept of the uncertainty principle nor of anything else quantum because it was reductionist. 'You took the whole and you broke it down into its parts and you analysed the parts and you never had more than the parts. Quantum things, on the contrary, are emergent. The whole is always greater than the parts. If, for instance, you take something simple like two paperclips. Each paperclip is a quantum system. If the two paperclips are joined together in Newton's system nothing magical happens. And indeed the particle-like properties do stay separate and keep their original identities, so that we still have two solid paperclips each with its own boundaries. But what Newton never discovered was that the wave-like properties of electrical particles will merge and will become one electric current. So two clips folded together represent a whole new quantum system. When you bring any two quantum things together, the whole acquires properties, has characteristics, has identity that wasn't there in the parts.

'We can feel this from our own experience – which is one of the things which led me into *The Quantum Self*. When we enter into an intimate relationship, we don't change physically but through the relationship we acquire some further potentiality, we acquire new characteristics, a new sense of being – this is what's attractive about relationships, it's why we get into them, because it evokes something in us we didn't feel was there before. It's a heady experience. Physical systems do it all the time; they enter into relationships and they acquire new properties.

'The fourth thing we should know about quantum physics is the relationship between the observer and the observed. In the old physics there was a sharp difference between the two – between subject and object. There is no such distinction in quantum physics. The observer is *part* of what he or she observes and the observed is part of what the observer is observing. This is because the quantum world changes with its surroundings, its context. It is always in dialogue with its environment – the context has a great deal to do with its identity – and the observer is of course part of that context. It still baffles scientists, but through experiment it has been found out that the act of observation collapses the wave aspect, the multiple potentiality aspect into the particle, the single actuality aspect. Observation collapses the wave function and nobody knows why. Some people think that consciousness does it, or gravity, or that it just happens spontaneously. But, whatever the cause, it happens when we observe and measure the system. So, something about the relations between observing reality and reality itself, changes reality.

'So, from these four differences we have the possibility of a whole different world view. The holism tells us we are all part of each other. The uncertainty tells us things are not fixed; there's room in this system for some kind of freedom. Indeed there's the possibility of freedom in quantum physics that there never was in the old physics. The emergence of quantum systems allows us to see the world as created, as surprising, as constantly unfolding. And the observer relationship tells us that we are in constant creative dialogue with the world around us. That we are partners in creation, not masters of it.

'The physicist David Bohm pointed out that there is a huge similarity between the way quantum systems behave and the way human minds behave. For instance, we can wake up with a vague train of thought and in our imagination entertain many possibilities but when we have to make a decision, when we have to focus, then we have to choose the particular. In our imagination we can entertain many possibilities all at once, even mutually contradictory ones. A quantum system in the brain would give us a physical basis for this because quantum systems are all over the place with many possibilities. So the question really is – is this eerie similarity between quantum processes and brain processes and the nature of the self just an accident or is there something to it? Increasingly people are now thinking that there's something to it.

'The particular kind of quantum system that has to exist in the brain if it's going to support consciousness is called a Bose-Einstein condensate. The thing about Bose-Einstein condensates is that they are the most entangled coherent structures in the physical world. Everything is overlapped with everything else. A laser beam is a Bose-Einstein condensate and that's why laser light is so incredibly coherent and you can do things like micro-surgery with it. It's as though all the molecules have got so overlapped with each other that they are just one molecule. The reason why people suspect a Bose-Einstein condensate must be the basis of human consciousness is because consciousness has this amazing unity. We are all being bombarded every moment by billions of sensory data – textile, thermal, visual, auditory and so on – and yet we don't see them in billions of pieces. It's one of the miracles of consciousness that we see the world as a unified picture. And beyond just the usual unification there is a noetic unification, a meaning unification. We know why we're here, we know what we're doing and we know who we are. So our whole world is unified.'

Without this unity and wholeness, Danah tells us, we could not experience the things around us in the way we do. Our whole experience of the world would be nullified. There would be no sense of self or other, therefore no decision-making or intentions. All the familiar features of our mental life would be missing. The unity is the most essential condition of our consciousness. Indeed it's so basic that most of us never give it a thought. And yet it's when we try to understand the unity that we see how truly mysterious consciousness is and why the physics of it have so far not captured it. There is nothing else like it known by the ordinary physics concerned with our everyday lives. The whole body of classical physics and all the technology that stems from it – such as computers – is about the separateness of things, about the different parts and the influence they have on each other across their separateness. It is not about the way we see the world as one.

The structure of reality is, for Danah, the most exciting and necessary exploration there could be. And essentially it is the exploration into the spiritual aspect of reality that attracts her most. And here quantum science has revealed the great and vast heart of consciousness – the vacuum.

The quantum vacuum underlies all existence. When physicists discovered waves and particles, and found that these waves and particles always transmute into each other in a sort of dance, they needed to find out what lay beneath it all. If particles and waves were manifestations, what were they manifestations of? A new branch of physics was born and according to this new science, all that exists – everything that we can see or measure – is a wave on an underlying vacuum, a 'ground state', just as waves undulate on the sea.

The vacuum cannot be seen and cannot be measured but its existence is now proven. It seems as though all existence is in constant interaction with 'a tenuous background of evanescent reality'. It is not that the universe is filled with the vacuum, but that the universe is 'written on it', or emerges out of it.

The quantum vacuum is very inappropriately named, Danah thinks, because it is not a vacuum in the sense that it is empty. Rather, it is the underlying reality – the basic, fundamental beingness of which everything else in the universe is an expression. After our universe was born in the big bang, there came into being space, time and the vacuum. We can think of the vacuum as a 'field of fields', she says, or as an ocean of potential. It is without any particles in itself but all particles exist within it as excitations – energy fluctuations. We can think of it in this way: if we lived in a world of sound, the vacuum would be like a drum skin and the sounds it made would be vibrations of that skin. 'The vacuum is the substrate of all that is.'

The exciting discovery about the nature of the vacuum, says Danah, is that one of the fields within it is now thought to be a Bose-Einstein condensate – a condensate with the same physics as our own consciousness. So when we try to understand our consciousness – where it springs from and what its purpose is – we can now believe that human consciousness is one of the potentialities within the vacuum. We might even have grounds to speculate that the universe itself is 'conscious' and that it has a basic sense of direction towards greater and fuller consciousness and coherence.

'If we were looking for a God within physics,' continues Danah, 'the vacuum is the closest we will find. The vacuum is the source of everything, the fount from which everything comes. Every existing thing is a wave on this vacuum. We are all waves on the same sea. This is how we relate to everything else in the universe, not only to each other. A speck of dust is no less an important excitation than a person – there is no hierarchy in quantum physics. There is a sense in which I am much more complex than a speck of dust. And there is another sense in which I, if my consciousness is a Bose-Einstein condensate, reflect that vacuum. I am like it, I am created in its image. Anything living, so physicists have discovered, has got a Bose-Einstein condensate in it, even bacteria. So, we people of the living world have something slightly closer in common with the vacuum than a speck of dust has, in that we not only issue from it, are waves upon it, but we also bear a direct likeness to it. But the whole world has emanated out of it, including the speck of dust, so every existing thing has a precious quality to it. Every existing thing is a possibility or a unique incarnation of the vacuum.'

This understanding of the nature of reality could bring about a deep change in the way we regard God or the spirit – not something on high and out of our reach, but a presence that is always there within us, underlying all we do. Danah sees the vacuum in this way and believes that everyone can understand such a concept, even if they know nothing of quantum physics.

'To say that human consciousness reflects the way we emerge from the vacuum does not need a degree in physics. You may understand it better if you know the physics but you don't *need* it. You can still make a shift in your thinking, a change of attitude, without knowing any physics . . . A great many sociologists, philosophers and writers have, of course, expressed deep dissatisfaction with [the older] mechanistic science and the culture it has spawned. But all too often these critics of mechanism then choose to ignore science altogether, or remain ignorant of the radically new discoveries and altered perceptions made possible by the new science. Often this leaves their intuitions without the more solid foundation that science could provide . . .

'Some people say that takes all the mystery out of things. It may take the mystery out but it doesn't take the awe out. I can have a tremendous sense of the wonder of reality even though it's not mysterious to me any more. This notion that knowledge somehow destroys wonder seems to me so ignorant, so medieval. How can we be frightened of knowledge? We were given brains to have knowledge. Why did we evolve to have this intelligence if we're afraid to use it to find out?'

Danah calls the quantum vision a way of life and in her books she explains the practicality of taking it seriously:

'There's a huge morality latent in what I'm saying. If you and I overlap, if you are a possibility sleeping within me, if we are excitations on the same vacuum, then you and I are one in some very real sense. So I am not my brother's keeper, I'm my brother. So my moral attitude towards you is one of treating you as I treat myself. And in the same way, the whole ethic of protecting the environment is there because the environment again is an expression of me, of my potentiality – it's stuff of my same substance, tissue of my being. So I would treat the environment with great reverence.

73

'But this is all a new way of seeing life and people are not going to come to this from the western paradigm of belief and of being led. There's a bit of this in all of us. We want someone – Big Daddy, God, or some strong leader – to come along and clear up all the mess. But this quantum way of life does not answer those needs. Instead it insists that each of us takes the responsibility.

'Are we mature enough to live in this way? I don't know. But it's the challenge of the times and if we don't meet it I think the planet won't survive with human beings on it. We have such enormous problems today. We simply can't go on as we have been doing. Take just the ethic of how we relate to others who are different from ourselves. We now live in a global reality where we impinge on each other all the time. In the streets we constantly meet people who are different from us. We can either hate them and react against them and fight with them or we can see them as expressions of our own possibility and love them and live with them. At the moment the world needs and requires the latter.'

Danah believes that if we can understand the way our consciousness works, if we can take seriously the particle and wave aspects, then our lives will become richer, more mature and happier.

The particle aspect means that we sense our apartness as people who experience life each from our own point of view; the wave aspect takes us up and weaves us into the being of others and indeed of all the world. These paired conditions are the circumstances that allow us to relate to others and to have them relate to us without our own personal integrity ever being completely isolated or exhausted. And it is this twofold state of being that enables us to become not only persons in our own right but also members of a community. Our twofold nature is why we feel a glow of homecoming and a sense of fulfilment when we find ourselves accepted into a family, group or movement that is bigger than ourselves.

Danah believes that in this way we are 'midwives to reality', acting as a bridge between the realm of potentiality and the world of actuality. Our imaginations supply us with endless possibilities but yet we must focus our thoughts and choose just one. In this way we bring that one to objective life, for there is something really there for us to pluck it from. Our imagination does not *create* the world, the world *exists* and when we take that one aspect of reality from its great ocean of potential, we are *discovering* it creatively, we are actualizing its potential.

The truth of quantum reality, Danah tells us, is an ambiguous one for it has an imperative – and that is for us to recognize 'the possibility of other possibilities'. But such ambiguity, such lack of definition, can be creative. In the physical structure of the brain from which consciousness arises it *is* creative because a self-organizing system needs ambiguity to function and thrive. Such a system as the human organism can run down if it becomes too static; and it can break apart if it becomes too chaotic. It must have a particular creative balance of order and chaos to function well – and that balance is an ambiguous one. Danah believes that it is essential we should cultivate the sort of maturity that can accept ambiguity and endless possibilities because then we can also accept with tolerance the vision created by others: 'It is a maturity that allows me to live in a complex and pluralistic society without losing my bearings.

'The wave–particle dualism in self or society is a powerful metaphor on which we can build a new model to transcend the individualist/collectivist divide, but I believe it is more than a metaphor. I believe that human consciousness really is quantum mechanical in its origins, and that the mechanics of this quantum consciousness *literally* give our minds, our selves and our social relations both a wave aspect and a particle aspect. The wave aspect is associated with our unstructured potential, with our spreading out across the boundaries of space, time, choice and identity. The particle aspect gives us our structured reality, our boundaries, our clearly defined selves, our ordered thoughts, our social roles and conventions, our rules and patterns.'

Danah feels that exploring the wave possibilities is an enlargement of the particle self and that we constantly long for such expansion. She takes the example of faithfulness in marriage.

During the seventeen years of her own marriage, she tells us, from time to time she has felt attracted to another man. On each occasion the attraction has held the promise of bringing out some aspect of her nature that she didn't know existed and this was such a heady experience that she even had fantasies of abandoning her family and running away with the new man. She has observed that such attractions usually happen at times when she is somewhat bored with her husband, and their relationship seems merely routine. But she has always told her husband about her feelings for somebody else and although the situation is highly uncomfortable and their conversations become painful because of implied dissatisfactions and unfulfilled expectations, nevertheless her husband always *listens*. And simply because of this listening something happens between them. In some way Danah comes to see that her husband actually possesses the quality she thought she had found in the other man. Neither he nor she had been aware he had that quality until they had talked about it. Indeed, the very honesty of their dialogue and their ability to confide in each other, evoked a potential that had been latent and waiting there all along and this new potential could enter their relationship. The urge to be unfaithful would leave Danah at once.

To understand ourselves in a quantum way helps us, Danah believes, to see that we have an infinite potentiality waiting to be aroused within us. This potentiality is called forth by the people we meet and the experiences we have. There is no limit to the potentialities or to the person that each one of us can be. We often feel this about ourselves but all too often have difficulty in feeling it about others. We lazily or indifferently take people at face value, cast them into roles and then treat them as though they had no further dimension. By forgetting to look, by taking for granted a relationship and making it habit-bound and routine, we trap ourselves and our partners. Then we may feel we want to evoke some new side of ourselves with somebody else. Such exploration of the self through others may be necessary when we are young but greater maturity brings with it the knowledge that potentiality for true growth lies within one committed relationship.

In our very diverse society it should be possible, with the help of the quantum vision, to discover a 'sacred' way of life, Danah believes. She points out that we may never again find the common sacred dimension within the structure of any particular one of the existing religions, particularly the western ones. 'We do not now nor, I believe, will we ever again live in a "Christian society", any more than Muslims can live in a "Muslim society" without ruthless repression and the denial of modernity, or Jews follow their ancient covenant in the same spirit while being members of wider society. We can do so only if we find our common roots in some dimension of reality that both undercuts and at the same time gives meaning to our differences. I believe we can find these roots in the quantum vision . . .'

We should be on the side of evolution, she feels.

'If anybody is going to help the vacuum to evolve, it is us existing humans. Instead of being masters, we should become servants of the universe, agents of the universe, co-creators of reality. The spirit should be one of service. We are unique possibilities rising up out of the sea of multiple potential. Each of us bears a responsibility.

'In the life of this universe, we're on about day three of a year – we're at the beginning of time. But if we don't sort ourselves out, we may be at the end of human time. Although it's true that even if we destroy ourselves, the whole evolutionary process will probably produce something intelligent again, nevertheless the main thing is, we ourselves are just starting out, we are the agents of evolution, and it's our job to be here and to know and to discover. We've now discovered quantum physics and we have to ask some philosophical questions, such as, what are its implications? How does this connect with that? What questions arise from it?

'The shift of the western paradigm – its common vision – must now be to move from answers to questions. To ask questions may be the most profound thing we can do. We should not expect to go on believing; there is nothing to believe in. The quantum vision means learning about the possibilities and how we can act on them. It's about transforming ourselves and transforming consciousness.

'The quantum vision is wild and beautiful in some ways, but people ask me how might we go about practising it and relating to it. I believe the first thing is to become awake and aware – to realize how much of our time we spend as sleepwalkers, on automatic pilot. We need to wake up and celebrate the diversity of life and of physical existence and to notice the sanctity of that grain of dust.

'And then there are practices such as meditation. You don't have to do any particular meditation, it's just a way to become quiet. I meditate when I walk, for instance. I notice each step I take, pay attention to the way my foot goes down on the ground, and then my walk becomes magical because I become aware of my movement through the land and of my contact with the ground, with the stones, and the whole place seems to come up through me.'

She believes that in her outer life she should try to be active. She should make the effort to be fully in contact with the wider world not only through family and friends but also through belonging to a group or association. One could say this is the opposite of the solitary religious path, for this means a putting aside of personal inclination in order to be fully involved with the world. It should mean involvement with politics too at some level and, says Danah, if there is no group of people available then she might think of starting one. But, above all, in whatever she does and at whatever level she acts, she must *listen*, she must enter into dialogue and she must do whatever she can to promote dialogue between others.

'*Every time that I try to understand another person's point of view it is a small religious act. It is also a small political act.*

'The dialogue between our various meanings, cultures, social groupings, etc. are the concrete steps in the unfolding process of the vacuum's evolution from potentiality to actuality. Thus there is a natural covenant between the vacuum and ourselves, between the source of all being and ourselves. This is a covenant between the vacuum and our social and political reality. The nature of this covenant grounds all our meanings in a wider sea of shared potential meaning. It lays on us the responsibility to express as much of this potential – develop as much of its pluralism – as possible.

'This covenant between ourselves and the vacuum is *sacred* because it is about the ultimate meaning of our existence. If we call the vacuum by its other names, God or Being or the Buddhist Void, this becomes more obvious. The vacuum is our common reality. It is the source of our being and of our being together. It is because the vacuum contains all potentiality and because the vacuum is within us that we carry the potentiality of the other within us . . .

'Through this new "quantum" covenant all our private meanings acquire a new, shared public meaning. Each becomes a creative partner in the shared public enterprise of evolution. We – you and I – become partners in this enterprise, not *despite* our differences, but *because* of our differences. We need each other fully to become ourselves, to evolve that "dance" which is our common reality; and evolution needs us to be different fully to realize itself. This . . . is a spiritual process, the basis of our deeper, shared meaning: our covenant.'

Marianne Williamson

'Love is what we were born with. Fear is what we learned here. The spiritual journey is the relinquishment, or unlearning, of fear and the acceptance of love back into our hearts. Love is the essential existential fact. It is our ultimate reality and our purpose on earth. To be consciously aware of it, to experience love in ourselves and others, is the meaning of life.'

For Marianne Williamson such an acknowledgement of the power of love was not an instant or easily acquired solution to the problems of her own existence, let alone the world's. The loving came to her as the illumination of her life after many years of stumbling about in the dark.

Marianne was born into a middle-class Jewish family in America. Her grandfather was an orthodox Jew and took her to the synagogue with him. 'I was very passionate about saying my prayers at night. My mother would come into my room and find me sitting up reciting my set prayers, which were a mixture of the Lord's Prayer and a Hebrew prayer.

'God was a very specific, literal, powerful presence. As a child I was absolutely convinced that if I forgot to say my prayers I would have a nosebleed – and I did. Once my parents had a friend who was going to have heart surgery and I had it planned to pray for him the night before. With a child's faith I was absolutely certain that my prayer would carry him safely through his operation. But when I went to bed that night I was so tired that I forgot to say my prayers. The man died. I felt absolutely sure that it was because of me.'

It is hardly surprising that during her teenage years she rejected such a God. She decided she could do without him altogether, certainly as a crutch, since he seemed unable to prevent catastrophes and she would not believe in him any more. 'I actually wrote God a Dear John letter. He obviously still existed for me psychologically if I had to write him, but I felt I had to give him all my reasons why the relationship wouldn't work any more.'

But somehow doing without God seemed to mean doing without

purpose and she found herself increasingly at odds with authority and unable to cope with her own life. She drifted into the drop-out society of the late sixties and early seventies and says, with frankness, that she remembers little of that time. It passed in a haze of experimentation with whatever was marked as forbidden or outrageous, and she looked for relief from her own lack of purpose in food, drugs and relationships. Her parents begged her to do something with her life but although she knew she was intelligent and had talent, she did not know how to apply it.

'There was a huge rock of self-loathing sitting in the middle of my stomach during those years, and it got worse with every phase I went through.' Yet as her pain deepened, so did her interest in philosophy and she read all she could find: 'Eastern, Western, academic, esoteric, Kierkegaard, the *I Ching*, existentialism, radical death-of-God Christian theology, Buddhism, and more. I always sensed there was some mysterious cosmic order to things, but I could never figure out how it applied to my own life.'

By her mid-twenties, she says, she was a total mess. She could not believe that the conventional idea of 'making it in the world' could be all there was to existence – and yet what else was there? In spite of all her reading, no other door had opened to her.

It seems that true despair is often a turning point. We come to the end of ourselves and there is nothing left – at least nothing that is recognizable by us in our black hole. But beyond this limited body-self is vast enlightenment and if we are able to perceive our limitations and look for 'the other', we will find it. Such has been the experience of many, including Susan Howatch. For her also there was too much superficial stimulation of the senses until her soul screamed for something deeper – and found it. For Marianne, it was her own personality that was defeating her: 'It wasn't drinking or drugs that was doing me in; it was my personality in general, that hysterical woman inside my head. My negativity was as destructive to me as alcohol is to the alcoholic. I was an artist at finding my own jugular. It was as though I was addicted to my own pain.' And then, one day, the moment came when she opened her eyes and saw a new life altogether.

But first of all she went through a bad nervous breakdown – 'the mess got so thick that all the king's horses and all the king's men couldn't make Marianne function again' – but the breakdown, she now believes, was an essential part in the opening up that led to her finding that new life. It humbled her deeply. She saw at last that of herself she was nothing. In all her battling with the demons of her psyche she had never before surrendered herself wholly, seeing with such clarity the futility of all her actions. And 'that's when your head cracks open and God comes in'.

She felt, she says, as though her very skull had exploded into thousands of pieces which, very slowly, began to come together again. And while her brain was so exposed, it was changed, as though rewired. She knew herself to be a different person. Such an experience is not unheard of during deep depression or breakdown. It is as though a natural healing mechanism breaks right through the old brain circuits and cuts the habit-formed connections in a way that no medicine from outside can do. It feels as though a compassionate and sublime energy has taken the brain into its own hands and shifted all the suffering pieces into a new and peaceful whole.

It was in 1977 that Marianne first came across the work that was to inspire her life and to complete the healing process within her. She tells us that she saw a set of blue books with gold lettering sitting on someone's coffee table and she picked up one of the books out of curiosity. It was *A Course in Miracles* and it had no named author but was produced by the Foundation for Inner Peace. But when she looked through it she found it full of Christian terminology and was put off by this. It was to be another year, with all its attendant misery, before she looked at the books again – and this time she knew at once that here was her teacher. And this time too she was able to accept the Christian terms because she could see that they were being used in ways that kept the essence while discarding the conventional and pious. They were more psychological than religious, 'challenging my intelligence and never insulting it'.

It is a truism that all things are born, grow, and die away but nevertheless it is difficult for most of us to appreciate this process when it applies to organized religions. They seem so monolithic, so self-perpetuating, but in fact unless their foundation is one of universal truth, they cannot be kept alive indefinitely. This is why we are now seeing empty churches and (at least in Britain) a real decline in the number of people calling themselves Christians. What is dying is

81

the formalized and ritualized culture and tradition which has little to do with the inner spirit, although many people confuse the two. The real Christianity is emerging in new ways and *A Course in Miracles* celebrates this.

The *Course* uses the term Christ, for instance – so Marianne tells us – in an esoteric and psychological way meaning 'the common thread of divine love that is the core and essence of every human mind'. And the title God is the source of that love, the energy of it that supports the world.

Marianne found the *Course* so revealing and came to study it so deeply that it was natural for her – rather as an extension of her own understanding – to begin writing and lecturing about it. At first it was in a small way but her audiences began to build up and as they did so she discovered that she felt more and more easy and unselfconscious as she talked about the *Course* until she could address an audience of a thousand without worry, talking to them in the friendly and immediate way in which she wrote her first book, *A Return to Love*. This book became an international bestseller.

But whatever stardom she has attained, she always remains true to the *Course* and to the one subject she feels we all need to learn about and can never know enough about – how to love. The *Course* itself contains 365 psychological exercises, daily ways of seeing the world with new perception so that each day becomes a miracle. The core of those miracles and the basic teaching is learning how to live in the world as a loving person. It calls itself a mind-training in how to relinquish our habitual thought system which is based on fear and to accept instead a thought system based on love. 'Love taken seriously is a radical outlook, a major departure from the psychological orientation that rules the world. It is threatening not because it is a small idea, but because it is so terribly huge,' says Marianne.

It is difficult to imagine the results of such love. Marianne points out that there would never be wars because we would not fight those we loved. Nor would starvation exist because it would be unthinkable not to feed people. Our love would keep the world from environmental damage and from the dying out of animal species killed by greed. There would be no more violence or oppression.

Taking love seriously means a complete transformation of our thinking. *A Course in Miracles* brought Marianne to notice that whenever she reached a loving perception of a situation, things worked beautifully. But when she did not things stayed stuck. She came to see that the mind's function is to practise love and if it does not do that, there is no wisdom. 'Without love, we might be active but we're hysterical.'

She sees love as an energy which people can feel, and can also feel the lack of. Few people have enough love in their lives and the world is consequently a loveless place where fear seems more real than love. In *A Course in Miracles* the true sin is that of 'loveless perception' which leads to fearfulness. But love can cast out fear and although shifting one's perception does not mean that every problem will automatically be solved, it does mean that the intrinsic source of problems, which is our consciousness itself, can be altered and the miraculous shifting can then work on what the *Course* calls the Causal level. Without this turn around of consciousness, all problem-solving is temporary and is a fix and not a healing.

'Loveless perception' is a remarkably accurate term for what most of us experience much of the time. Our ability to blind ourselves to the wonder and beauty of the world about us is phenomenal. We scurry about the world intent on the ideas in our head and pay almost no attention to the underlying depth and meaning of all that surrounds us. 'Loveless perception' must surely be when we see nothing but ourselves and all that pertains to ourselves; whereas 'loving perception' is when we drop that self-centredness and see the world afresh with open eyes.

Marianne points out that, according to the *Course*, our thought is the Cause and what we experience is the Effect. If you don't like the effects in your life, then you must change the nature of your thinking.

She tells us that there are no limits to love and no edges where one part breaks off and another begins, for we are all totally interconnected. 'There's actually no place where God stops and you start, and no place where you stop and I start. Love is energy, an infinite continuum. Your mind extends into mine and into everyone else's. It doesn't stay enclosed within your body.'

Thus the energy of love is infinite and the mind in each one of us extends into all other minds and theirs into ours. Danah Zohar makes the same point when she describes the wave function of the mind. The view that in this conscious universe all minds affect each other and also the world about us is nowadays thoroughly supported by quantum physics and by environmental studies.

But the *Course* takes us into a realm which is even beyond the new science. It believes that there is only *one mind*. 'The concept of a divine or "Christ" mind is the idea that, at our core, we are not just identical, but actually the same being. "There is only one begotten Son" doesn't mean that someone else was it, and we're not. It means we're all it. There's only one of us here.'

We can think of ourselves as individual waves on a vast ocean, which is the same source for us all. We can't become separate from the ocean any more than we can separate ourselves from each other. And the ocean, says Marianne, is love. We are upheld by and living in that oceanic energy of love. She also uses the analogy of a wheel. 'If you identify with the spokes and with their positions on the rim of the wheel, then we're all different spokes. But if you identify with the hub, where they all originate, then we are all one, with the same source. Jung spoke about the collective unconscious: the notion that there's a realm of mental energy that we all share. "One mind" takes that concept one step further, that not only is the Id stuff of our mind identical but that in fact it is the same mind. The *Course* takes the concept that all minds meet at the source part of the same mind. Therefore at the deepest level we are one.'

The idea that there is just one mind in all of us is a difficult one for many people to accept, because it brings forth an underlying fear of having no identity, of being a clone in some Aldous Huxley scenario. We value our individuality. We do not seem to be the same as everyone else.

Yet if we look more deeply, we can see the truth of such an extraordinary claim. First, there is quantum physics again and Danah's description of the vacuum of which everything in the world is an excitation. This is essentially the same description and the same discovery: that there is one source from which everything arises, that that source is the same for all of us, and that therefore we are of one being.

Also, in Eastern religions, there is the same belief. The one source is often called the Self, because there is thought to be no dividing line between the Self and the individual self. Zen Buddhism illustrates this understanding with a light-hearted story about some squashes ripening behind a temple. One day a fight started among them and the noise was so fierce that the head priest came out. He made them all sit in zazen and once they were calm, asked each one to put its hand on top of its head. When they did so, they all found a weird thing on their heads. It turned out to be the one vine from which they all grew. They said, 'Actually we're all tied together and *living just one life*. In spite of that we've been arguing. What a mistake!'

The Zen comment is that we are certainly living as a small individual body called I and we *think* this small individual body is our only self, that it is all there is. But the Self as the reality of life is never just this individual body. 'Common sense tells me that the power which makes my heart beat and sends the blood flowing through my body and allows me to breathe regularly is not something I can bring into being or even control. It completely transcends my thoughts. But because this power comes from beyond my thoughts, can we say this power is not I? As long as this power is working within me, it is indeed the reality of my life. It's not only these kind of physical functions, but the same is true for ideas and thoughts which arise in my head, too. Looking at the contents of these ideas and thoughts, it certainly appears as though they are my thoughts and ideas. But it is surely so that the very power that allows me to work out these thoughts and ideas is a transcendent power beyond my thoughts. Yet it is also the reality of the life of myself. So we can say that while the reality of the life of the self exists beyond the small individual I, yet it also exists as the power which breathes and gives life to this small individual I' (Kosho Uchiyama Roshi).

We should surely ask ourselves why it is that we remain stuck within our body and give little, if any, thought to the transcendent source that lives in us? Why do we choose to live only from the small self and not from the infinite greatness of God? Marianne believes that 'there is a tendency in our minds, which can be amazingly strong, to perceive without love'. From childhood onwards we imbibe the belief that there is no other power but the individual self, that we are self-powered, autonomous, separate creatures whose worldly progress is the only thing of any importance. And that progress depends on our being able to compete with all the other separate beings. This fractured way of looking at existence naturally comes to be based on fear. First of all, the basic fear that we are nothing in ourselves; and then, arising from that deep existential fear, come all the other fears: of insecurity, competition, of not succeeding, of not being able to hold the one you love, and so on. Marianne tells us the *Course* term for this whole network of fear-based perceptions – all of which arise from that initially false belief that the only power resides in the small self and that each small self is separate from all the others – is the ego. During this century psychology has given that term a good number of interpretations, but the *Course* uses it in its original Greek way as the dominating idea of the small self.

The ego is not only fear-based, but it is anti-love. Love threatens its survival for love points beyond it to a greater understanding of existence. When we live only from the ego, we separate our thinking from love and, as Marianne points out, that means that we turn our power against ourselves.

Was there ever a time when humanity lived without ego? We don't know. And yet there is a nostalgia, a feeling of loss when we talk about the Garden of Eden or Atlantis or other mythological perfect places from which we were 'expelled'. We left those places to inhabit a world based on delusion. The *Course* calls this moment of departure (often re-enacted over and over again in our lives) our 'detour into fear' or 'separation from God'.

Marianne points out that the ego has a pseudo-life of its own and is like a gravitational force-field drawing us away from love. If we want a Devil, the ego is it. Like a silver-tongued one, she says, it will cleverly point us in the direction of self-centredness. 'The ego doesn't come up to us and say, "Hi, I'm your self-loathing." It's not stupid, because we're not. Rather, it says things like, "Hi, I'm your adult, mature, rational self. I'll help you look out for number one." Then it proceeds to counsel us to look out for ourselves, at the expense of others. It teaches us selfishness, greed, judgement, and small-mindedness.'

A great mystic of this century, Simone Weil, also saw the ego as gravity. Indeed she saw the whole everyday world as a world of gravity, of sheer necessity and ego-power, which has the effect of pulling us downwards into material density unless in moments of grace we forget the self and sense the presence of God: 'Gravity is the force which above all others draws us from God. It impels each creature to seek everything which can preserve or enlarge it. Psychologically it is shown by all those motives which are directed towards asserting or reinstating the self, by all those secret subterfuges (lies of the inner life, escape into dreams or false ideals, imaginary encroachments on the past and the future, et cetera) which we make use of to bolster up from inside our tottering existence, that is to say, to remain apart from and opposed to God.'

But we should remember, says Marianne, that what we think we're giving to others – judgement, anger and so on – is in fact what we are giving to ourselves because we are one and there is no division between us. If we choose fear instead of love, we deny not only to the other but also to ourselves 'the experience of Paradise', because if we abandon love we will feel it has abandoned us.

What is the alternative to an ego-dominated existence? There *is* an alternative, because we have been given free will. We are not automatons. We are conditioned but our conditioning can be seen for what it is and allowed to drop away. 'There would be no hope for the born, the manifest and the time-bound,' said the Buddha, 'if there were not that which is unborn, unmanifest and timeless.' Liberation does exist and is there, waiting for us. The *Course*, Marianne tells us, teaches that the way to freedom and the answer to the ego and its world of fear is the Holy Spirit.

The Holy Spirit is the force of consciousness within us that delivers us from fear when we consciously ask it to. God can't force his way into our thoughts because that would be encroaching on our free will. But if we call on God, the Holy Spirit will work with us on the Causal level and transform our thinking from fear to love. The Holy Spirit is the drive towards wholeness within us. It's impossible to call on the Holy Spirit in vain, she tells us, because he is built into the framework of our personhood. And he comes in many forms. Marianne reminds us that we may not recognize him but he is there just the same in what suddenly gives us a new perspective. It can be a poem in the newspaper, or a talk with a friend or a popular song. We often condemn teenagers for their noisy, insensitive music but this may well be how the Holy Spirit is reaching them at their stage of development for, as Marianne says, he is the 'inexorable drive towards wholeness that exists within, no matter how disoriented or crazy we get'.

The Holy Spirit corrects our perception by guiding us to view life in a different way. But this may not always be a comfortable process. Calling on the Holy Spirit means that we will be made to grow. The *Course* believes that the purpose of our life is to grow into perfection. If we happen to be rather imperfect it is likely that we will get some painful and difficult situations bringing us to our knees. Marianne herself found this over and over again, in particular with failed relationships, which showed her the ways in which she could *not* love. For the Holy Spirit is no respecter of any emotion less than total unconditional loving.

Marianne believes that the Holy Spirit has a curriculum for everyone which is exactly individualized for each person so that every situation or encounter can be used for his purposes. The Holy Spirit is the go-between operating between the true and perfect self, which is universal and with which we are one, and the 'worldly insanity' which is our usual perception. 'He enters the illusion and leads us beyond it.'

However dire our fate – and we only have to look around us in the world to see how very dire the ravages of war can be or the menace of AIDS – when the Holy Spirit is invited into these situations, he will use them as points of individual growth through which they may be eradicated from the world by changing the way in which we think.

Our everyday life is our spiritual path although many people never realize this. The Holy Spirit, says Marianne, is a force in our minds that knows our perfection (which we have forgotten) and that also enters into our world of fear and delusion, using our own sad experiences to remind us of who we are: 'He does this by showing us the possibility of a loving purpose in everything we think or do. He teaches us to see love as our only function.'

The *Course* sees Jesus, Buddha and other enlightened beings as 'evolutionary elder brothers', the spearheads of a mutation in humanity. For the laws of evolution have shown us that a species will develop in a certain way until that way proves to be no longer viable. Then the species, if it is to survive, must adapt to new conditions. This is when a mutation occurs and it only happens to a few individuals at first. A new line of evolution, better adapted to survival, begins to emerge, and the descendants of those who have mutated are then the survivors.

It is obviously necessary that we, as a species, should mutate and our way to survival, Marianne believes, is to create a world of love. 'A thoroughly loving person is like an evolutionary mutation, manifesting a being that puts love first and thus creates the context in which miracles occur. Ultimately, that is the only *smart* thing to do. It is the only orientation in life which will support our survival.' In this sense, the enlightened people of the past have shown us our potential and pointed the way for us to follow.

The universe supports and upholds us physically and supports our emotional and psychological survival as well. But just as we are polluting the outer world, so we are polluting our relationships if we abuse them with unloving attitudes. The laws of the universe describe the way it works and are not dependent on whether we believe in them or not. Abuse of these laws doesn't mean that we are bad, merely that we lack intelligence. 'We respect the laws of nature in order to survive. And what is the highest internal law? That we love one another. Because if we don't, we will all die. As surely as a lack of oxygen will kill us, so will a lack of love.'

The power that holds galaxies together, says Marianne, can take over from us when we allow it to and will do a much better job than each of us on our own could effect. But the choice is ours. Surrender to that power means giving up our attachment to results. The very surrender means that our so-called control over outside events has to be relinquished and we must learn to become more concerned with inner happenings.

Making the choice to love means that we change the structure of our lives, for when loving is the real purpose and value, then all the things we've thought would make us happy but didn't are seen as external searchings for something that is always internal. Looking for happiness in outside objects is, says Marianne, the meaning of idolatry.

Certainly most of us can see that to desire material objects and to believe in their happiness-granting power is indeed worshipping false gods. And indeed most of us can surrender many things fairly painlessly. However, as Marianne points out, 'Everything we don't care that much about – fine – God can have it. But if it's really really important, we think we better handle it ourselves.' But in fact if we surrender that which is most important to us, we find it is taken care of best.

Marianne tells us that she used to feel she could not afford to let go because she was sure she was unimportant to God. Finally she realized that the God she had been believing in was an unlikely, capricious one and the real one is not at all like that, because the real God is an impersonal love for all life: 'My life is no more or less precious to Him than anyone else's. To surrender to God is to accept the fact that he loves us and provides for us, because he loves and provides for all life. Surrender doesn't obstruct our power; it enhances it. God is merely the love within us, so returning to Him is a return to ourselves.'

What Marianne emphasizes is that there is at all times another dimension to the world, the liberating dimension of love. If we muffle ourselves in the everyday existence, if we think we know and believe that this is all there is and will ever be, we are psychologically mutilating ourselves. There may be moments of love but there will also be moments of despair because our dependence is on changing outer phenomena and not on the unchanging love of God. Then we may ask for a miracle. However, the *Course* tells us that although miracles do happen, they are more likely to happen involuntarily to those who have developed a loving personality and live in accord with themselves, believing not that they are small and inadequate creatures on this earth but that they are full with an abundance of love and with the power to give it.

For we are not just randomly put here, Marianne believes, but we have a mission and it is to save the world through healing it by the power of love. The world badly needs healing, people know this, and many pray for it: 'God heard us. He sent help. He sent you.'

The *Course*, says Marianne, believes that the old adage 'many are called but few are chosen' means that everyone is called, for God's call is universal and reaches every mind at every moment, but few want to hear it because they prefer the loud voices of the outer world. So if we feel we are called, how should we proceed? Our task is continually to encourage a greater capacity for loving and forgiving in ourselves and to do this through what is called 'selective remembering'. We are to make a conscious decision to remember loving thoughts and to let go of negative and fearful ones.

This is what the *Course* means by the word 'forgiveness'. Forgiveness is very important to the philosophy of the *Course* and the word is not used in the traditional way but in a much wider and more liberating sense.

We usually 'forgive' when someone feels guilty for what they have done. But in the *Course* it is important to remember that there is no guilt, for only love is real and our forgiveness is unnecessary. There is of course guilt for whoever is feeling guilty, but the 'forgiver' sees through the guilt to the reality of the primal innocence beneath. The *Course* takes the unique position that love is all-encompassing and that therefore fear (and all its attendant emotions, such as guilt), which seems to be the opposite of love, does not truly exist – for what is all-encompassing can have no opposite. So the maxim of the *Course* can be expressed in three lines:

> Nothing real can be threatened.
> Nothing unreal exists.
> Herein lies the peace of God.

Our job, says Marianne, is to see through the illusion of guilt to the sinlessness that lies beneath it. We should see with new eyes and we should extend our perception beyond the mistakes and the terrible errors that we observe with our physical perception to the original wholeness which only our hearts can reveal. And since all our minds are interconnected, at some level the healing we give through the correction of our perception is also a healing of the entire racial mind. 'The practice of forgiveness is our most important contribution to the healing of the world,' says Marianne.

And we must practise it, for focusing on someone else's guilt is a sure way of hurtling down with the force of gravity to a generalized fear and hatred. The ego loves to judge, to find fault, to see everything as inferior, wrong, to be despised. From time to time the newspapers report on a murdered child, for instance, and there is a national wave of intense loathing for the murderer. But it is ourselves we are loathing, for we are one with the murderer as well as one with the child.

The Vietnamese monk Thich Nhat Hahn says:

I am the 12-year-old girl, refugee
    on a small boat,
who throws herself into the ocean after
    being raped by a sea pirate,
and I am the pirate, my heart not yet capable
    of seeing and loving.

We must focus on the basic innocence, Marianne tells us, rather than on the guilt. Focusing on the innocence sets us free to work on the liberation of the murderer as well as ourselves. 'Forgiveness is the key to inner peace because it is the mental technique by which our thoughts are transformed from fear to love.' Every relationship and indeed every thought can lead us towards either love or fear, either heaven or hell. Heaven is the awareness of perfect oneness, of true alignment. Hell is the consciousness of no oneness, no alignment, no love, only fear.

Forgiveness, says Marianne, is the real means by which we move towards heaven. Forgiveness is practised in the *Course* as 'selective remembering', which is a conscious focusing on love and letting everything else go. It is not at all easy to do because the ever-present ego demands the energy of negativity and 'presents the most subtle and insidious arguments for casting other people out of our heart'. The ego would have the whole world be guilty; the Holy Spirit knows that it is innocent. Selective remembering means a conscious effort to bring the Holy Spirit into every relationship and to 'deliver us from the temptation to judge and find fault'.

To illustrate this Marianne recounts an occasion when she was in Europe with her family. She and her mother were often irritated by each other and although they were trying to get along together on this holiday, they were not succeeding. Each wanted to change the nature of the other. Marianne kept looking to the *Course* for help but each time she took up the book it opened at the same place and said: 'Think honestly what you have thought that God would not have thought, and what you have not thought that God would have you think.' She realized she should examine her thoughts to see where they were not aligned to God's, but she found she didn't want to do this. Her ego called out for support in its battle with her mother. She did not want to be told, she discovered, that her real mistake was in the way she was thinking.

'Finally, glancing across St Mark's Square in Venice, I looked closely at my mother and said to myself, It's true. God's not looking at her and thinking, Sophie Ann is such a bitch. As long as I chose to see her that way, as long as I was not willing to give up my focus on her errors, I could not be at peace because I was not sharing God's perception. As soon as I saw this, I released my tense fixation on what I perceived to be her guilt. From that point forward, the situation began to shift. Miraculously, she was nicer to me, and I was nicer to her.'

As Marianne points out, it is fairly easy to forgive and think well of people who have done nothing to us, but our best teachers are the ones who really make us angry because they show the exact limitations of our willingness to forgive.

But perhaps sometimes a grievance is justified. It is very hard, says Marianne, to try to eliminate our perception of wrongdoing. And indeed how we should react to crime is a big ethical decision. By not making a judgement and meting out punishment, are we condoning acts which should not be condoned? Marianne herself has often felt 'Well, *somebody's* got to uphold principles in this world. If we just forgive things all the time, then all standards of excellence will disintegrate.'

But this feeling, she has come to understand, is not a correct perception. 'God doesn't need us to police the universe.' Condemning someone is not in the end helpful to them. 'Shaking a finger at them' does not get them to correct their ways, whereas 'treating someone with compassion and forgiveness is much more likely to elicit a healed response'. Forgiveness, she says, creates a new and better context in which someone can more easily change.

It is a hard choice for all of us, but a choice nevertheless that has to be made between behaviour derived from fear and behaviour inspired by love. People, says Marianne, behave unlovingly when they've forgotten who they are. Our job is to keep remembering and not to fall asleep and 'dream of our brother's guilt'. We should keep awake and it is through our wakefulness that we have the power to wake him.

Calling on the Holy Spirit is the way to stay awake. It may be beyond our power to change our perceptions of a situation, but by calling on the Holy Spirit to do it for us, we receive the help we need. Marianne presents the possible situation of somebody whose husband has left her for another woman. The victim can't change the people involved, but she can ask to see the situation differently. She can ask for peace through a change in her perceptions. 'The miracle is that, as you release judgement of your husband and the other woman, the pain in your gut begins to subside.'

Relationships – all relationships with everything in the world – are assignments for us to work on, Marianne believes. They are part of a vast plan for our enlightenment, 'the Holy Spirit's blueprint by which each individual soul is led to greater awareness and expanded love'. The meaning of our lives is to become open vessels of God's love. We are here on earth to be the physical representatives of a divine principle.

So we have a meaning and a destiny to turn away from the perception of fear and to turn towards the perception of love. If we once make this move in all sincerity then we need do nothing else but remain there, for the Holy Spirit will give us the talents and also the opportunities to use those talents throughout our lives.

Marianne's work on *A Course in Miracles* has enhanced her sensitivity, particularly towards the difficulties that women face in what is still a male-orientated world. Her second book, *A Woman's Worth*, has been devoted to clarifying both through her own and other people's experiences the nature of women's problems and how the *Course* can shed light on them. She explores women's insecurity, and also their dependency on loving and on being loved, in an increasingly fragile and loveless world. She sees the nature of love as usually being misunderstood and projected on to the wrong vehicle – a man or a career – when it should be turned inwards to enhance the inner life of the woman and all about her. But she also sees that women have a particular gift of loving which needs to be upheld.

A woman in love can do anything, she says. She can manage a family and run a business, cook, make love, look marvellous – and even lead a nation. But if she is not in love the energy diminishes. 'Women need to be in love: with themselves, with a man, with a child, with a project, with a job, with their country, with their planet, and – most important – with life itself.'

A Zen master once said that it is possible and not only possible but desirable, to fall in love with everything – even an orange. 'If you can truly marry this day, then you can experience true love with any man or woman.' Falling in love with everything in life is to add what Marianne calls a mystical third to the man–woman relationship, for what you are really falling in love with is the spirit of creation, the Holy Spirit. You are creating love instead of fear. Falling in love with life creates the desire to serve it and the Holy Spirit will then give us the means by which we will be able to serve, says Marianne. What we actually do is not so important.

'Our power doesn't lie in what we've done or even in what we're doing. Our power lies in our clarity about why we're on the earth. We'll be important players if we think that way. And the important players of the coming years will be the people who see themselves as here to contribute to the healing of the world. Everything else is trivial in comparison ... Whatever our gift is to God, however humble it may seem, He can turn it into a mighty work on His behalf. Our greatest gift to Him is our devotion. From that point of power, doors open. Careers blossom. We heal, and the world around us heals.'

Annie Dillard

What I aim to do is not so much learn the names of the shreds of creation that flourish in this valley, but to keep myself open to their meanings, which is to try to impress myself at all times with the fullest possible force of their very reality. I want to have things as multiple and intricately as possible present in my mind. Then I might be able to sit on the hill . . . where the starlings fly over, and see not only the starlings, the grass field, the quarried rock, the viney woods, Hollins Pond, and the mountains beyond, but also, and simultaneously, feathers' barbs, springtails in the soil, crystal in rock, chloroplasts streaming, rotifers pulsing, and the shape of the air in the pines . . .

What do I make of all this texture? What does it mean about the kind of world in which I have been set down? The texture of the world, its filigree and scrollwork, means that there is the possibility for beauty here, a beauty inexhaustible in its complexity, which opens to my knock, which answers in me a call I do not remember calling, and which trains me to the wild and extravagant nature of the spirit I seek.

The valley Annie Dillard writes about is in Virginia, where Tinker Creek flows, and it is the inspiration for her most famous book, *Pilgrim at Tinker Creek*, which won the Pulitzer Prize. She is the pilgrim and her journey is both outwards and inwards. She is a naturalist, staying close to nature and trying to learn its habits and directions through observation. At the same time she is also a mystic, contemplating what she looks at with a new and different perception. Central to her vision is the sense of the world as 'itself'. Her appreciation of it, and of the sacred always immanent within it, means a constant letting it be by acknowledging that everything has its own life – a life which may not fit her preconceived model of it at all.

She tells us, for instance, of an afternoon when she was standing on a beach off the Atlantic coast of Florida. It was low tide and to her astonishment she saw a hundred big sharks passing the beach to feed near the mouth of a tidal river. As each green wave rose above the churning sea, the long bodies of the twisting sharks could be seen illuminated within the wave. As the waves rolled towards her and broke on the shore, the sharks would disappear. And then a new wave further out would begin its rolling swell, turning and heaving, and the sharks would appear again, caught in the water like scorpions in amber. 'The sight held awesome wonders, power and beauty, grace tangled in a rapture with violence.'

Such a sight caused her to query her understanding of the world and to ask the question, what is going on? If these tremendous events are random, without meaning or significance, then what is it in us that they ignite? She believes we can't know. 'Our life is a faint tracing on the surface of mystery, like the idle, curved tunnels of leaf miners on the face of a leaf.' Somehow we must widen our viewpoint, take in the whole landscape of life, really look at it with full attention and describe what's going on. Then we can at least begin to 'wail' the right question into the darkness of our ignorance, or, if we find the right answers, sing out our praise.

'Taking the wider view' and 'looking at the whole landscape' means for her a continuing struggle to be aware – or at the very least to be present to what is happening and not adrift somewhere in her thoughts. 'Beauty and grace are performed whether or not we will or sense them. The least we can do is try to be there.'

She feels about what she observes that it is both 'connected' and 'other'; and it's because she is certain that everything, including herself, shares in the same amazing life that she can allow herself to be entranced by the 'other', by the myriad differences, although this very entrancement is not by any means automatic. The world contains many gifts and surprises waiting for us to discover; in fact it is 'studded and strewn' with pennies flung bountifully from a generous source, but the trouble is, are we going to be enchanted by a mere penny? For instance, it's possible, she says, to wait motionless on the bank of a stream to watch for a ripple spreading on the water and then to be rewarded by the sight of a muskrat paddling out from its den. But will that sight grip the heart or will it be counted as an insignificant penny only? And will we who are watching go away disappointed after all, our expectations unfulfilled?

This question highlights the dilemma that most of us face. In a world of self-survival, where is our limited energy to be placed? Do we have time in an action-packed life to watch for a muskrat? And if we see one, will it be a reward of unmistakable wonder or will we be longing for it to disappear so that we can go on to the next job or the next fascination? Throughout Annie Dillard's work there is the feeling that for life to be worth living it must be unrushed, based on inner silence and space, where living in the present is the most important act, where sounds can be really heard and sights really seen. 'I walk out. I see something, some event that would otherwise have been utterly missed and lost; or something sees me, some enormous power brushes me with its clean wing, and I resound like a beaten bell.'

In this way what she experiences becomes more vivid to her than she is to herself – the barrier of self is lessened and she no longer stands in her own light. Contrary to many mystical teachings, consciousness itself, she tells us, does not prevent us from living in the present. In fact, it is only to a heightened consciousness, an increased awareness, that 'the great door to the present opens at all'. It can even be helpful to use words and describe things to oneself because it enforces the memory of what is taking place. We need to call attention to what is passing before our eyes, otherwise it is often lost.

But *self*-consciousness, the return to the self, does blur the experience of now. Self-consciousness is the one state that blocks all the rest. As long as Annie can lose herself in a tree, for instance, she can then absorb its leafy breath or even estimate the amount of lumber it would make. She can pick the fruits of the tree or boil tea on a fire of its branches, and the tree will stay itself, a tree. But the minute she starts reflecting on herself doing any of these activities – as though she were looking back at herself over her own shoulder, as it were – the tree will no longer exist in the same way, it will disappear from her unselfconscious awareness as though it never was.

She believes that self-consciousness is essentially a city curse because, cooped up in a city, one lives mostly through the reactions of other people. Although the city offers the vitality of human companionship and endless stimulation, the stimulation itself is like a drug and afterwards leaves one drained. It is a place for novelists, not poets. She finds that being innocent is a happier condition. Innocence sees the object as it is and finds it satisfying just for itself. 'What

I call innocence is the spirit's unselfconscious state at any moment of pure devotion to any object. It is at once a receptiveness and total concentration . . .'

Devotion to any object depends on a real encounter with that object. It means the action of being present with it in a total way, and that encounter is denied to many of us because, as with the penny, we don't consider it worthwhile. The world is taken for granted and we let it all slip past us without even seeing it, far less encountering it. But for Annie the encounter is a true and essential source of happiness and wonder. Her books teem with encounters on many levels – plants, animals, insects – she brings everything to our attention, even to the contents of the pond water under her microscope: 'I don't really look forward to these microscopic forays: I have been almost knocked off my kitchen chair on several occasions when, as I was following with strained eyes the tiny career of a monostyla rotifer, an enormous red roundworm whipped into the scene, blocking everything, and writhing in huge flapping convulsions that seemed to sweep my face and fill the kitchen.' She looks, she says, as an exercise in morality – something that may not be enjoyable, but should be done. The microscope she peers through is like the small box of scriptures that Jews wear round their necks to remind them to keep the law, for her microscope is a constant reminder of nature's laws and the facts of creation that she would really rather ignore. But 'these are real creatures with real organs leading real lives, one by one. I can't pretend they're not there. If I have life, sense, energy, will, so does a rotifer.'

Because Annie Dillard's mysticism has led her to the natural world, her language is always of creation where, to her, the divine is immanent. This way of exploring and expressing the spiritual is more usual in America than in Europe and she is frequently compared to Thoreau. In England there have been nature mystics such as Wordsworth and Keats, Matthew Arnold, Richard Jeffries and Kenneth Grahame, but none apparently so deeply and totally committed to the exploration of natural life as the Americans. Perhaps the English, in the small amount of country left since industrialization, see it more as a garden, a place for tranquillity and contemplation; whereas Americans know nature as wild and vast and untamed, not always beautiful and frequently dangerous. The great value of

Annie Dillard's reflections lie in the fact that she never loses sight of the savagery in nature and is always prepared to look at it with unblinking honesty.

One such occasion was brought about by what started off as a casual walk beside an island in the creek. Frogs were jumping in every direction and after walking for a while she became better at distinguishing them both in and out of the water. They were active everywhere but when she came to the end of the island she could see a small green one that was half in and half out of the water and not leaping at all.

Its immobility surprised her. She crept closer and still it didn't jump. At last she knelt down on the winter-dead grass and felt strangely lost and dumbstruck as she stared at the frog, now so close. He was very small and his eyes were wide open but dull. Even as she looked at him, he began in an odd way to crumple and sag. His eyes went dead, their spirit suddenly extinguished. His flesh seemed to evaporate, leaving his skin empty and drooping and even his skull appeared to fold in on itself, collapsing like a tent with its props knocked away. He was shrinking in front of her eyes and she watched the taut glisten of his skin round the shoulder bones rumple up and fall away. Very soon some of the skin, as shapeless as a pricked balloon, lay floating in folds on the water like coloured scum. She felt appalled and bewildered by such a terrifying and monstrous occurrence. And then she noticed a menacing oval shadow hovering in the water behind the drained frog. But even as she looked closer, the shadow glided away and the empty frog skin began to sink and disappear.

She realized the killer was a giant water bug. She had read about them but never seen one. It is a huge, heavy beetle which eats frogs and can even eat fish. It hooks its victim between great forelegs and then paralyses it with enzymes injected in a stabbing bite. It only takes the one bite. The poison it injects dissolves the victim's flesh and bones and through the puncture it has made the beetle sucks out the whole body, which has now become a juice.

Annie Dillard knows, of course, that many animals eat their prey alive and that 'every live thing is a survivor on a kind of extended emergency bivouac'. But at the same time she feels that we are all created, that there is a God at the source of creation, and she asks the question that Allah asks in the Koran: 'The heaven and earth and all in between, thinkest thou I made them *in jest*?' She feels this is a legitimate question. 'What do we think of the created universe, spanning an unthinkable void with an unthinkable profusion of forms? Or what do we think of nothingness, those sickening reaches of time in either direction? If the giant water bug was not made in jest, was it then made in earnest?'

Indeed, what kind of God would make such cruelty and pain? She believes the answer can only be a mystery – although equally mysterious are beauty and light and the grace that takes one by surprise and carries one away by its wonder. But the divided nature of creation, the existence of cruelty, pain and fear as well as enchantment, continue to haunt her and it is this honest acknowledgement of the dark side of life that gives her work its power. Many people nowadays write about reverencing nature, about being one with the trees and communing with the plants, but very few actually study what they are talking about or admit to the savagery of creatures against each other in the battle for survival. Because she wants the whole truthful picture and not just the pretty part of it, Annie Dillard continues to look and search and observe and to carry her observations into the realm of an existential questioning spirituality. And lingering always at the back of her mind is the worrying problem of free will. Does it exist? Or are we, in whatever we do, automatic and conditioned in ways we know nothing about? Free will wins in her philosophy, but it is not always a sure win.

She tells us she was standing one day, feeling thoroughly lost and depressed, her hands in her pockets and her gaze directed towards Tinker Mountain. Suddenly she saw what looked like a Martian spaceship. It was whirling towards her and the sun shone on its movement like a flashing light. She watched, transfixed, and saw it rise up just before it would have touched a thistle. It hovered briefly, twirling, in one spot and then whirled on until at last it found a resting place. She discovered it in the grass and saw that it was a maple key, one winged seed from a pair. She greeted it with pleasure, threw it up into the wind again and watched it fly away 'bristling with animate purpose' and not at all something at the mercy of conditions, fallen or windblown or pushed about by the unheeding currents of convection that follow the world's movements as they must;

but much more like a living creature with strength and muscle, or, indeed, a creature that could respond to another wind – the wind of the spirit, which bloweth where it listeth and which illuminates and lifts up and gently eases down. 'O maple key, I thought, I must confess I thought, O welcome, cheers . . . If I am a maple key falling, at least I can twirl!'

The maple key led her out of her sense of existential depression towards a feeling of free will, but the depression itself might lead us to ask if perhaps she had never experienced the particular sense of the sacred that other writers in this book tell us of, when time is suspended and the immediate present is suddenly transformed and a new freedom that is spiritual is born. But in *Pilgrim* she tells us of a moment of just such transcendence. She had been thinking about the fact that when surgeons first knew how to operate on cataracts in the eye they operated on dozens of people who had been blind since birth. These people were like newborn babies and, until their eyes grew used to seeing, they mostly just saw different kinds of brightness. One girl that Annie took note of saw a tree with lights in it. Annie herself longed to find this tree.

She searched for it, she tells us, through the summer orchards and in the autumn woods, in the winter countryside and the spring meadows for years. Then one day when she was not thinking of it at all and was simply walking along beside Tinker Creek, she saw it. She saw a cedar she knew, in which the mourning doves roosted, and it was 'charged and transfigured, each cell buzzing with flame'. She stood there on the grass and the grass itself had lights in it. It seemed as though the grass was on fire and she saw it with a totally focused and yet utterly dreaming gaze. 'It was less like seeing than like being for the first time seen, knocked breathless by a powerful glance.'

The flame of the fire died down but the power of it stayed with her. The lights in the cedar went out, the colours faded away and the cells of the tree lost their luminosity and disappeared from her view. But she herself 'was still ringing'. All her life she had been a bell but until that revealing moment when she was 'lifted and struck' she had never realized it. Since then she has only rarely seen the tree lit up in that same way. 'The vision comes and goes, mostly goes, but I live for it, for the moment when the mountains open and a new light roars in spate through the crack, and the mountains slam.'

This was a revelation that affected the whole of her life, for it brought her the certainty that the divine does exist. It gave her a reference point for the rest of life and she became aware that increasingly she knew a different kind of seeing from the usual botanical observation which filled her days.

Such a way of seeing is one which means letting go, she tells us. 'When I see this way, I sway transfixed and empty.' This different mode of seeing is like walking without a camera, whereas her usual botanical way necessitates a camera. When she walks with a camera at the ready she goes from one scene to another, reading the light on a calibrated meter. But when she walks without a camera 'my own shutter opens, and the moment's light prints on my own silver gut . . .'

However, it is not possible just to go out and expect to see in this way, for she would fail and send herself mad with trying. All Annie can do is try to stop the chatter in her mind, the endless inner babble that distracts her from seeing. Indeed, we all know the commentator in our heads who never stops telling us what we should or should not like, and who brings up endless visions of what happened yesterday or last week whenever there is the smallest crack in our concentration. She would like to gag the commentator but, she points out, this is a discipline needing a lifetime of dedicated struggle. It is the aim of all the contemplative religions and many have devised practices, such as breath-counting or mantra, to silence the commentator and to achieve an uncluttered mind.

Annie Dillard calls such an unclouded mind and transformed seeing the pearl of great price. 'If I thought that he could teach me to find it and keep it forever I would stagger barefoot across a hundred deserts after any lunatic at all.' But although the pearl may be found, it must not be searched for, she says. The literature of the mystics throughout the ages reveals this fact above everything, that it comes unexpectedly, and as a gift, as though one finds oneself facing in the right direction on the right day. Although it also comes in time to those who wait for it, even the most ardent practitioners and adept meditators may be taken aback with wonder when the illumination suddenly arrives.

Annie describes how, for instance, she might return from a walk on one particular day and be so much in practised touch with the countryside that she has discovered where the killdeer nests near the creek and knows the hour the laurel comes into bloom. But she can return from the same walk a day later and be so unexpectedly entranced that all her practical knowledge is forgotten and she barely knows her own name. She can't cause the light, she says (any more than we can with our own efforts gain the gift of illumination). All she can do is try to put herself in the path of its beam. She reminds us that in deep space it is possible to ride on the solar wind. Light, whether it is particle or wave, has energy and force. 'You rig a giant sail and go. The secret of seeing is to sail on solar wind. Hone and spread your spirit till you yourself are a sail, whetted, translucent, broadside to the merest puff.'

Such a spreading of the spirit and letting go of the self, she calls a very ordinary mysticism and she believes that any meaningful effort at all requires such a commitment. But her commonplace understanding and knowledge are needed too:

Knowledge does not vanquish mystery, or obscure its distant lights. I still now and will tomorrow steer by what happened that day, when some undeniably new spirit roared down the air, bowled me over and turned on the lights . . . I saw the cells in the cedar tree pulse, charged like wings beating praise. Now, it would be too facile to pull everything out of the hat and say that mystery vanquishes knowledge. Although my vision of the world of the spirit would not be altered a jot if the cedar had been purulent with galls, those galls actually do matter to my understanding of the world.

Annie Dillard is one of those rare people who do not divide the sacred from the everyday. For her it is all one. She brings a self-free attention to the mystery and also a sense of communion with things as they are. Each thing has its own life, it has a living presence which can speak to her if she can only listen. And she is completely committed to listening; it is her passion and her service to the esoteric Christianity she believes in. And in order to listen as well as she can, she uses all the tools at her disposal. She encounters creation at every possible level. She learns to understand the physical nature of things through biology and botany. She reads for her own pleasure about the great expeditions of the world – Captain Cook to the Antarctic,

Darwin to the Galapagos Islands – and she goes to these places herself. She learns the way islands are formed and the structure of the land. She is an explorer in every dimension.

In the Ecuadorian jungle she reflects that the whole point of going to such a unique place as the Napo River is not so much to see what is spectacular as to learn what is there. We only come once to this planet, she believes, and so we might as well get a feel of what it is like, sense the 'fringes and the hollows where life is lived'. And when she goes to the Galapagos Islands, it is for the animals that she makes the journey. She wants to observe the strange shapes that soft protein can take, she longs to apprehend their reality and above all she wants to greet them.

She feels she should witness what she encounters as if she were newly born, or as if her eyesight had been given to her afresh, as it was to the cataract patients and the girl who saw lights in a tree. And so she tries to accept everything as it presents itself, in an effort to let her body do the seeing. She should be able to know, she thinks, an innate connectedness to life, a sense of beingness, preconceptual and pre-reflective, which must still exist within us, although it has been forgotten and overgrown by our rationality and self-consciousness. In her book of her childhood, *An American Childhood*, she reflects that when every fact has left her brain – the name of the President and names of cities where she has lived and then her own name and what it was she looked for, as well as the faces of her friends and the faces of her family – when it has all finally gone what she will be left with, she thinks, is topology: 'the dreaming memory of land as it lay this way and that'.

This dreaming memory is the body's knowledge, its relatedness to the body of the land. She feels that this knowledge existed before the mind knew anything and will exist after the mind forgets, but as well it is also there throughout the middle. It underlies the way we live and our knowing even though the conscious mind may resist it.

Animals may possess this knowledge but she is very aware that for all of us, for all creation, there is beneath the apparent freedom of design and pattern in the world an evolutionary predetermined. Even though she is satisfied that free will exists, and even though she feels joined to the land by her body's memories, yet she cringes and quails at, for instance, the prolific and eggy world of the insects in which life is very cheap indeed. 'I don't know what it is about fecundity that so appals. I suppose it is the teeming evidence that birth and growth, which we value, are ubiquitous and blind, that life itself is so astonishingly cheap, that nature is as careless as it is bountiful, and that with extravagance goes a crushing waste that will one day include our own cheap lives.' When we look, she says, at the myriads of insect forms we can see that nature will try anything once. Apparently no form, from the praying mantis to the tiniest ant, is too fantastic and no behaviour too bizarre. If organic compounds are being made, then let whatever combines combine. 'If it works, if it quickens, then set it clacking in the grass, there's always room for one more.'

She notes what a lavish economy this is, where nothing is lost but everything is spent, including ways of behaviour as well as of form: 'the mantis munching her mate, the frog wintering in mud, the spider wrapping a hummingbird, the pine processionary straddling a thread. Welcome aboard. A generous spirit signs on this motley crew.'

Nevertheless, in spite of her distress at the cheapness of existence, she does not lose sight of the transcendent way of being she was shown when she saw the 'tree with lights'. But she is aware that such moments cannot be the whole of her life and that perhaps there will always be a tension between knowing about the world and merging with it.

She tells us that one day she stopped at a gas station in Virginia. The friendly gas attendant gave her a cup of coffee and she stepped outside, alone except for a small beagle puppy who followed her. Suddenly she became aware of the marvel and beauty of the moment, the soft folds of forested hills, the clouds, the sunset. She could smell loam on the wind and she sat down on the kerb with her coffee beside her. She patted the puppy and gazed at the hills. She felt herself fully alive.

'This is it, I think, this is it, right now, the present, this empty gas station, here, this western wind, this tang of coffee on the tongue, and I am patting the puppy, I am watching the mountains.' But as soon as she had breathed the word 'I', she found she had lost the moment. She could no longer see the mountain or feel the puppy. She felt she had become opaque, like the pavement she was sitting on. But at the same instant that the perfection disappeared, she also realized that the puppy was still squirming on his back under her hand. For him it was still the same event and nothing had changed. She reflected how ironic it is that self-consciousness, which is recognized by all religions as separating us from the transcendent, is as well the one thing that divides us from the world and our fellow creatures. 'It was a bitter birthday present from evolution, cutting us off at both ends.'

But the premature finishing of that sublime moment was not the most important thing because it would have ended anyway. 'I've never seen a sunset or felt a wind that didn't,' she says. 'No, the point is that not only does time fly and do we die, but that in these reckless conditions we live at all, and are vouchsafed, for the duration of certain inexplicable moments, to know it.'

Although seeing the tree with the lights in it had been a very different experience from stroking the puppy, because 'the steady inward flames of eternity' had shone in the tree whereas at the gas station the mountain was lit by 'the familiar flames of the falling sun', yet on both occasions she had felt 'This is it, this is it; praise the lord; praise the land. Experiencing the present purely is being emptied and hollow; you catch grace as a man fills his cup under a waterfall.'

She tells us of an author, Stephen Graham, who described that sense of the purely present in his book, *The Gentle Art of Tramping*. He wrote: 'And as you sit on the hillside or lie prone under the trees of the forest, or sprawl wet-legged on the shingly beach of a mountain stream, the great door, that does not look like a door, opens.'

She had thought, Annie tells us, that because she had seen the tree with lights in it, 'the great door' must be the door that opens to eternity. But now that she had found the purely immediate present in the moment when she patted the puppy, and felt the particular enchantment of the senses, she also discovered that the door to the tree with lights in it was not opened *to* eternity but *from* eternity. It shone its timeless light on the tree but the tree was a real one, the cedar that she knew. So the door from eternity opened on to time – and, indeed, where else would it open on to? In a similar way the incarnation of Christ, she reminds us, with its unlikely and somewhat absurd emphasis on exact date, time and place, is called by its sincere believers 'the scandal of particularity'. 'Well,' says Annie, 'the "scandal of particularity" is the only world that, in particular, I know.'

And it is that particularity, lit by the timeless, that she celebrates throughout her books, bringing us ever closer, as she is brought herself, both to the immediate present and to the cosmic. We feel her own multiplicity of experiences – of enchantment, awe, and also uneasiness and fear as she leaves the human-centred view of nature. She describes encounters in such a way that we can sense the very organism, even if only in our imagination. Focusing our attention, she helps us become open to the presence she is with.

In 'Living Like Weasels' she takes us to a pond where she frequently sits on a fallen mossy tree-trunk to watch the lilies, the carp and the birds. A yellow bird flew past and caught her eye:

I swivelled around – and the next instant, inexplicably, I was looking down at a weasel, who was looking up at me.

Weasel! I'd never seen one wild before. He was ten inches long, thin as a curve, a muscled ribbon, brown as fruitwood, soft-furred, alert. His face was fierce, small and pointed as a lizard's; he would have made a good arrowhead. There was just a dot of chin, maybe two brown hairs' worth, and then the pure white fur began that spread down his underside. He had two black eyes I didn't see, any more than you see a window.

The weasel was shocked into total stillness just as he was coming out from under a dense, wild rose bush four feet away. Annie too felt the same shock and was equally stunned into stillness while she was still facing backwards on the tree-trunk. Their eyes locked and 'someone threw away the key'.

She never knew what shattered the moment but the weasel vanished under the wild rose again. 'I think I blinked. I think I retrieved my brain from the weasel's brain, and tried to memorize what I was seeing, and the weasel suddenly felt the yank of separation, the careening splashdown into real life and the urgent current of instinct.'

She wonders what went on in his brain, to which she feels she was somehow plugged in – or, rather, they were both plugged into another tape simultaneously. 'What does a weasel think about? He won't say. His journal is tracks in clay, a spray of feathers, mouse blood and bone; uncollected, unconnected, loose-leaf and blown.'

This sudden instant of shared life has come without warning, as a gift, and she contemplates what she might learn from such an encounter:

I would like to learn, or remember, how to live . . . I don't think I can learn from a wild animal how to live in particular – shall I suck warm blood, hold my tail high, walk with footprints precisely over the prints of my hands? – but I might learn something of mindlessness, something of the purity of living in the physical senses and the dignity of living without bias or motive. The weasel lives in necessity and we live in choice, hating necessity and dying at the last ignobly in its talons. I would like to live as I should, as the weasel lives as he should. And I suspect that for me the way is like the weasel's: open to time and death painlessly, noticing everything, remembering nothing, choosing the given with a fierce and pointed will.

Reflecting on this strange and unsettling encounter, she realizes that she and the weasel share a universe. But for this to be apparent, her own private universe must be changed. Can she imagine a different world in which both she and the weasel exist together *without self-consciousness*?

It should be possible, she feels, because we are all free and can live in any way we want. She thinks of religious vows of poverty, chastity, obedience and silence, which are taken by choice. The thing to do is to stalk your calling in a way that an animal stalks its prey, she tells us – a skilled and supple way – and then to look for the most sensitive and vital area and plug yourself into that pulsebeat. This, she says, is not attacking, not fighting, but discovering, through yielding to the single necessity of your life. She points out that a weasel does just that – he doesn't 'attack', because he yields at every moment to the single necessity of his life. He lives as he is meant to live with the freedom of single-mindedness, of having no choice.

To find that which is your calling in life, your one real and great necessity, is a spiritual and psychological need which everyone has. Having found that one commitment which takes priority over all others, do we then follow it single-mindedly and unselfconsciously to the end? Sadly, many of us are so muddled about ourselves that we fail to find even the one calling and perhaps by the time it is revealed we are hopelessly entangled in the net of superficial life. And very often we don't have the courage to do as Annie suggests and 'grasp your one necessity and not let it go, to dangle from it limp wherever it takes you'.

This is the way both she and the weasel must follow – she by her own choice and it by necessity. But despite their shared path, she cannot follow him all the way but must be true to her human life, which includes language and self-consciousness.

And her human life must learn to accept a greater reality of which she is a part. Even though the natural world seems to exclude any human meaning or significance, as does an earthquake or a cloudburst, Annie Dillard sees that this is part of the mystery and it does not deny the greater reality. She is certain that the way to live as a human being is to acknowledge the mystery constantly and at all levels and not to try to solve it, while at the same time remaining faithfully open to whatever presents itself, to the encounter with the other.

The philosopher A N Whitehead sought for a way to understand the numinous, the sense we have of the sacred as we feel it in natural surroundings. He talks of 'the brooding presence of the whole in its various parts'. For Annie Dillard too, the whole is in the parts and the sacred fills the particular. The dualism that many of us feel between our own subjective human consciousness and an objective world 'out there' is done away with when the world is seen as subjective and, in its own way, conscious. She quotes John Cowper Powys: 'We have no reason for denying to the world of plants a certain slow, dim, vague, large, leisurely semi-consciousness' and she adds, 'The trees especially seem to bespeak a generosity of spirit.'

The revelation in the last few years that the earth is a living organism has brought about in many people a new consciousness of themselves in relation to the earth and a new awareness that it is no longer just an object, any more than we are just objects. Quantum science too has melted the boundaries between object and subject and we now know that we are sharing in the subjectivity of the world. By grounding ourselves in this knowledge it is possible for us to lose our sense that we are in opposition to life, that we are 'alien' and 'foreign' to the world. We can forget ourselves and feel a oneness with the planet and all its manifestations, a oneness with the mystery of which the universe is a part. At the same time, our role is not only to accept such divine self-forgetfulness and to be blissfully swept away by it beyond the limitations of the self, but also to be humans with our own special gifts and roles to play; to use our self-consciousness (given to us by nature) to serve the earth and all that is on it and in it. We should use words, we should use thoughts, that is our contribution to the evolution of our universe.

Annie Dillard explores a moment of consciousness in this way. She is both self-forgetful and self-aware. She is sitting under a sycamore by Tinker Creek.

I am really here, alive on the intricate earth under trees. But under me, directly under the weight of my body on the grass, are other creatures, just as real, for whom also this moment, this tree, is 'it'. . . I might as well include these creatures in this moment, as best I can. My ignoring them won't strip them of their reality, and admitting them, one by one, into my consciousness might heighten mine, might add their dim awareness to my human consciousness, such as it is, and set up a buzz, a vibration like the beating ripples a submerged muskrat makes on the water, from this particular moment, this tree. Hasidim has a tradition that one of man's purposes is to assist God in the work of redemption by 'hallowing' the things of creation . . . Keeping the subsoil world under trees in mind, in intelligence, is the least I can do.

This is perhaps the true commitment of her life – to experience on the one hand the mystery which goes beyond everything we can know or understand, and on the other to cherish and serve all that she encounters with every human gift she possesses, by bringing it into her consciousness and paying full attention to it once it is there:

What else is going on right this minute while ground water creeps under my feet? The galaxy is careening in a slow, muffled widening. If a million solar systems are born every hour, then surely hundreds burst into being as I shift my weight to the other elbow. The sun's surface is now exploding; other stars implode and vanish, heavy and black, out of sight. Meteorites are arcing to earth invisibly all day long. On the planet the winds are blowing: the polar easterlies, the westerlies, the northeast and southeast trades. Somewhere, someone under full sail is becalmed, a trapper is maddened, crazed, by the eerie scent of the chinook, the snow-eater, a wind that can melt two feet of snow in a day. The pampero blows, and the tramontane, and the Boro, sirocco, levanter, mistral. Lick a finger: feel the now.

Vivianne Crowley

───────

> In caverns deep the Old Gods sleep,
> but the trees still know their Lord,
> and it's the Pipes of Pan which call the tune,
> in the twilight in the wood.
> The leaves they dance to the Goat God's tune,
> and they whisper his name to the winds,
> and the oak tree dreams of a God with horns,
> and knows no other King.

When she was twelve years old Vivianne Crowley, author of the above lines, started a witches' coven at her school.

'It may have been from the *News of the World* but somehow I got the idea that there were witches, that they worshipped the old gods, and joined together in covens.'

Vivianne was a devout Catholic at the time and she says it was almost as though her left brain thought Catholic while her right brain was going off into some completely different world. The girls at school were keen on the idea of a witches' coven but asked what they should do.

'Well, we'll dance about a bit. And then we ought to have an initiation ceremony,' Vivianne suggested.

They went down to the bottom of the school grounds and danced in a circle, chanting various sounds. For the initiation ceremony, Vivianne stood with her legs apart and her arms outraised in the pentacle position.

'Take it in turns to crawl through my legs,' she told the girls, 'and then each of you will be reborn.'

After they had done so, the girls began to feel energized and empowered and Vivianne was not sure what to do next. But the question was solved by a summons from the headmistress, who was receiving complaints about the noise from the occupants of the big houses bordering the school grounds. The coven had to be dissolved; but the idea of it did not leave Vivianne's head.

Indeed, her childhood up to then had led her more and more surely to this point. She was brought up on a farm at the edge of the New Forest and her most vivid encounters were with trees and animals and the heather-filled spaces she explored. She was six when she first felt a pull towards another dimension of existence and it came about through what is nowadays called an out-of-the-body experience.

'It started to happen when I went to bed. I would get out of my bed and go to the window and then it seemed as though I flew out. Instead of everything being dark, it was a kind of daylight but not like ordinary daylight – everything was bathed in a golden light. I didn't realize that this wasn't ordinary everyday waking consciousness and it seemed completely natural. I just went to the window, got out of my body and then I was flying around.

'I was aware of beings or presences, but with no substantial shape. I called them fairies but they weren't small; they were tall beings. It seemed as though I played a lot and as though I could see the same woodland I saw in the day but differently as though it was glowing in some way with a soft diffuse colour, as though one were looking through a gold filter. Leaves and trees and flowers no longer seemed solid but were crystals of coloured light.'

The first time it happened, Vivianne returned to her body and when she got up in the morning proudly told her mother that she could fly. Her mother advised her to eat her breakfast. She tried jumping from a fallen tree in the wood, spreading her arms and expecting to rise off the ground, but her feet began to hurt and she gave up, realizing that she could fly at night but not in the day.

These out-of-the-body experiences seemed, she says, to change her everyday waking perception as well. 'When I went to play in the woods it seemed as though everything was alive, as if the trees had awareness – in fact everything had awareness. I felt I wanted to merge with it and I found childish ways of doing it. I stood in the muddy little stream that meandered through the wood and tried to become one with it; or lay on my back gazing at the sky and then I thought I could feel myself merging into the earth. And I would take my lunch into the branches of a tree and sit there in the greenness, feeling the wind on my face. That particular tree had been split by lightning and a lot of ivy had grown over it. I would dress myself in the ivy and then put my foot into a V-shaped cleft torn out between the branches, which responded to the wind and opened and closed over my foot. When my foot was imprisoned I knew I was one with the tree and was riding with it in the wind. I would listen to the sound of the leaves, their mysterious rustling, and I would forget for a while which was the tree and which was myself. And I always felt a presence within the air about me, an energy I could not put a name to.

'I had much freedom as a child; much more than is possible to many now. I could spend hours at a time in the woods, coming home only to eat and to give adults the reassurance I knew they needed that all was well. Sometimes, if my friend was with me, we would be out all day and would take our lunch and eat it in the treetops; but more often than not she could not come, for she lived too far away, and our nearest neighbour was a Gypsy woman who lived in a caravan in the copse, with thirty cats and a daughter who was wilder than I. Not even I played with her.

'And being alone, I did not wish to be disturbed; so when people came to walk in the wood, I would hide myself so that they did not see me. I learned to walk silently and to merge with leaf and tree and sometimes to "disappear myself", so that I would move without moving. A Shaman would understand this, and some who know me now have seen it done, but I can't really explain it so as to teach it; save only to say that first one is in one place and then in another a little distance away, and something has passed through the brain very quickly, like two arrows crossing in flight.'

Many people have moments in childhood when they are aware of unusually enhanced perception and very often these memories are clear and unobstructed by later events. They seem particularly connected with the countryside and a feeling of belonging to nature. Kathleen Raine, the poet, remembers for instance the moorland in the north of England where she was sent as a child during the war, and her account in *Farewell Happy Fields* is similar to Vivianne's:

Tea over, I would run away to the moors behind; running, for the place I loved was a long way from the Manse. I ran up one slope of heather, and down a crag – a small, grass-grown crag – then up the next long slope to a second crag, wilder, and higher, and rockier, with dry sedge and hard polypod ferns splitting the rocks apart with their growth . . . and on to a tiny ledge that was my secret shrine; or something between a shrine and a hare's nest.

. . . here I sat like a bird on her nest, secure, unseen, part of the distance, with the world, day and night, wind and light, revolving round me in the sky. The distant and the near had no longer any difference between them, and I was in the whole, as far as my eyes could see, right to the sunset. The wind and the rain were like the boiling elements in a glass flask, that was the entire earth and sky held in my childish solipsist mind. The sun, the stratus clouds, the prevailing wind, the rustle of dry sedge, the western sky, were at one. Until the cold evening, or the rain, or the fear of the dark drove me to run home for safety to the less perfect, the human world, that I would enter, blinking as I came back into the light of the paraffin lamp in the kitchen.

Often it seems that it is the feeling of oneness with natural life – with grass and trees and sky – which seems to bring about a transcendence of everyday preoccupations. Another account reflects this:

When I was young I lived in the country. Trees and wind and grass mattered very much to me, especially the wind. When the branches of the great beech trees were swaying, or when clouds were blown across the moon, or when the wind was soft and moved through long grass, I felt sure there was a wonder and a mystery and all the world was somehow full of a meaning which I couldn't really understand and couldn't reach. But I desperately wanted to know the heart of that meaning and I had an intense longing to break through and to enter that marvellous world of light and wind and movement, to be one with it. I was sure that I truly belonged to it and that it had a great deal to do with a feeling I called the Presence, which seemed often to be there when I was alone in the fields and woods.

These words are echoed by Flora Courtois, another person with a vivid childhood, who says:

Even now I remember the feeling as a small child that all things about me, the people, the animals, trees and flowers, my dolls, my

plate and spoon, all participated with me in one vivid reality . . .
Often I felt in magic communion with other living things. Some of
my earliest memories are of rescuing drowning insects from a small
pond, of escorting small spiders from the house so they would not
be killed, of lying on my stomach in a neighbouring field, raptly
absorbed in the busy life of the tiny creatures under the giant grass
blades.

Such experiences, even to a young child, can give a sense of direction – often towards poetry and writing – and can form the basis of
a life-long commitment to the spiritual. In Vivianne's case, one
pointer after another led her to her life as a High Priestess of Wicca,
the ancient Pagan religion of witches.

One of the influences that pointed her in that direction was her
love of ritual. About the time that her out-of-the-body experiences
faded away, her Catholic grandmother came to stay and took her to
church. After her grandmother left, Vivianne decided there was something good about the Mass that she wanted to follow up. She was
seven and managed to cycle to the nearest church but Mass had
already started when she arrived. She crept in but was so small that
she could not see what was happening at the altar, and because it
was still said in Latin she could not understand it either. So Catholicism took a back seat again, but not for long.

The family moved to another village and at her new school Vivianne met two Italian girls. They were Catholics and Vivianne told
them she thought she might be one too. In that case she should go to
church with them, they said. So on Sunday they met her and took
her to Mass – to a church which was attached to a monastery. This
time she was taken to the front and so was able to see what she
describes as 'the amazing spectacle with the incense, the flowers, the
candles and the wonderful singing of monks. And then I was off! I
felt transported into the state of oneness or "otherness" again.

'So then I felt that the presence I had known in the woods was
also here in the church. I hadn't thought of the experience in the
woods as religious and I didn't have any deities at all, but now I
decided it *was* religious and I started to attend catechism classes.'

But she never gave herself completely to Catholicism, even so.
The God of the Catholics was somehow not her God. She would be

reminded of another world and would long to step into it again, back into the woods and the oneness. Other visions came to haunt her. Climbing the road up a steep hill, she found a strange shining stone: 'I turned it over and there was that stopping in time and space which occurs when we first see the one we are to love, or when there is great danger; for on the other side of the stone was the face of a goat. I took the stone home and it seemed to me a sacred thing, a thing of power; so I made an altar for it in my bedroom and covered the altar with a cloth and brought a vase of wild flowers and sat and looked at the stone until it was evening.'

Another very haunting vision was that of a stag. At school the children were asked to write a poem. As though it had been waiting to be summoned, Vivianne saw in her mind a stag come walking out of the woods. Although she was in a classroom, the stag seemed to come up to her and look at her and, as with the stone, she felt that here was an emblem of power. She felt the stag to be protective and very blessed, and the same golden light she had known when she was out of her body seemed to stream from its antlers. The image stayed with her for a long time and she knew it was part of the 'other world'.

However, the Catholic association was still in motion and she enjoyed it and in due time was confirmed. A priest suggested that she might have a vocation to become a nun and this too seemed a good idea for she was sure she had a vocation for *something*. When she was fourteen the family moved to London and although Vivianne wondered what she would do without trees and the countryside, nevertheless she was by then concerned about her education and was pleased to be able to go to the school she chose, which was a convent. She had never actually met a nun before and wanted to know if it was right that she should become one, because by this time she was actively thinking of it. But when the headmistress in her interview asked her what she would like to do in her life, she found she could not say she wanted to be a nun after all. It was not true any longer. But she loved the school. 'We used to pray all the time, every morning and afternoon and before each lesson. I was as high as a kite!'

A turning point in her life came when a missionary gave the school a talk not on Christianity, but on Buddhism. She learned to her surprise that there were more Buddhists than Catholics in the world. But the Catholics were saying they were the only right religion. Surely God couldn't want all those Buddhists to think the wrong thing. That would be ridiculous! At this point her Catholicism reinterpreted itself and she saw that there was no absolute, no definitely 'right' path, but lots of paths all equally good.

The school was run by a Belgian order of nuns who were feminist and progressive in their thinking and who included one or two Wicca rituals in their prayer-making, although Vivianne was not aware of that at the time. What she did feel, though, was a gradual loosening of her ties with Catholicism while she was at the school and this was emphasized, shortly before she left, by a talk with a priest, who told her she should follow her own conscience rather than religious dogma. It was another turning point in her life. She decided to take this advice and from then on put Catholicism behind her.

Vivianne never forgot the wonder of the countryside. It haunted her so much that by the time she was sixteen she felt quite desperate for the solitude of the forest and for the feeling of presence she knew when she was among the trees. London parks were not the same at all and she seriously wondered how she was going to go on living surrounded by concrete, and where her strength would come from if it could not come from the green energy of trees.

She realized that she must find such energy within herself and for the next few years she turned inward, into her imagination and her thoughts, and away from the streets about her. She longed to find a deity she could be at one with and wished she could see the stag again, believing it must have been some sort of god. She began to have strange visions and these accompanied her throughout her time at university.

One day she saw in a vision, perhaps drawn from her Celtic forebears, a tall red-haired chieftain, wearing a golden torc around his neck. He was clothed in a many-coloured cloak and rode a white horse with silver on its bridle. A standard-bearer rode before him, holding aloft a banner depicting an eagle on a green field, for the chieftain, she understood, honoured the Green Lady of the Meadows. A band of warriors, all brightly clothed, rode behind the chieftain. Somehow Vivianne knew that he was not one of that band, for although he had led them into many battles to free the people from their oppressors and had commanded the tearing down of the halls of the rulers who had abused their power, yet he was a stranger to them. They were a small and dark race and he in his size and red-haired majesty had seemed a god to them. They would have bowed down to worship him but he did not want this and told them they should worship the Great Spirit which unites both gods and men, and they should not give their worship to a mortal king.

It seemed to Vivianne that this vision of the king was of the same sort as that of the stag, he and the stag were the same, and for a long time she could not understand what this really meant. Then it came to her that worship of a man was wrong and that she would never be able to find her God in such visions. But another vision came to her and this time it was of a woman. The woman came in a dream. She had black straight hair down to her waist and grey-green eyes like the sea. In the dream she came out of the North, walking across the waves and ice floes towards Vivianne. She came as a Goddess, with glittering eyes, and Vivianne was in fear and awe of her.

Afterwards she realized that each successive vision had led to the next. First, as a child, she had known a God in trees and then in the goat-stone, and then as the antlered stag. Then he had appeared as a man, a king, and then she realized that he was none of these but was 'the breath of the Universe'. She felt he came at last as spirit but was within the world as the spaces between things and that which both binds the molecules and sets them free. And the Goddess who had come from the North was the Goddess of the Sea and could be found within the sounds of the waves. Such visions brought her to realize that the old deities of Paganism had always been there for her and she decided to commit her life to finding out their ways.

. . . in this journey of the spirit, I and others still walk that steep uphill road where I found my goat-headed stone . . . And all our religious edifices, which serve first as staffs to help us on our way, in the end become crutches which we must discard . . . And the doctrines which we espouse and which we hold dear are only smooth shining stones which we pick up on the road and place in our baggage. With each new dogma and doctrine, the baggage grows heavier, until we discard these pebbles, one by one, leaving them on the roadside for others to find and carry a little further. And in the end we have need of neither doctrine nor creed, nor to name that which we worship – for it is beyond all images and words. And who but a fool carries a stone to a mountain?

To fully establish her spiritual commitment, Vivianne found that she had to leave university after her first year. She could not concentrate on intellectual development, the call of the gods was stronger. She trained for three years as a priestess and then as a High Priestess in the Wiccan tradition. It was only then, at the age of twenty-two, that she felt free to go back to university and attend to her intellect. She then took her degree and after that a doctorate in psychology. With more training she became a psychotherapist, and she married. In due course she met others who felt as she did about the Pagan roots of the spiritual journey.

So what is Wicca? To its followers it is a religion equal to any other. They call it the Old Religion because it is based on ancient, possibly prehistoric and certainly pre-Christian, worship of the divine as it is manifested in the earth, the sun and the moon. Wicca bases its rituals of worship on the two fundamental life forces, female and male, and personifies them as Goddess and God. Both are given many names and forms, but at the same time it is recognized that 'all gods are different aspects of the one God and all goddesses are different aspects of the one Goddess, and that ultimately these two are reconciled in the one divine essence'.

It is by way of the Wicca rituals that every follower can participate in that one divine essence – and perhaps an outsider might say that the rituals of any religion, if they are sufficiently profound, will lead to the divine essence and therefore what is different about Wicca? The difference lies – at least to some extent – in the fact that Wicca uses natural magic as an integral part of the religion.

Vivianne tells us in her book *Wicca* that all people have within them psychic powers. Such powers, when used passively, lead to states such as clairvoyance. But they can also be used actively to make things happen and that is magic. She says that most people who enter Wicca have actually no more ability in clairvoyance and magic than the average person and nor is it necessary. The capacity of the ordinary person is more than ample when that person learns to use it. Most of us, she says, do not use one tenth of the capacity of our minds and much of Wiccan teaching is about training and developing our potentialities until we are able to make magic.

To become a follower of Wicca is not like joining the Church of England, where there is an established following and a priest to conduct the ceremonies. If you become a Wicca member, you are initiated into the priesthood at once and considered part of it. A woman is initiated as a priestess and witch and a man as a priest and witch. You then have the authority to perform the rituals and exercises for your own spiritual development. Do you join others in worship? Emphatically yes, but Vivianne points out that Wicca is not a religion suitable for everybody, but more the way of the few – albeit an increasingly large few. Wiccans are finding that more and more people would like to join them, for they offer a thorough spiritual training to develop self-knowledge and understanding. Vivianne sees some of Wicca's aims as similar to a spiritually orientated psychotherapy, although the two are not exactly equivalent as Wicca is a religion, the main purpose of which is worship of the gods, whereas psychotherapy is devoted to personal development. However, religion implies and needs personal development, and the small groups which operate on an intense level of commitment draw people to just that – to Wicca's personal approach to spiritual discovery. Perhaps too they are attracted by the fact that it provides new and natural ways of worship. For one of the hardships of our materialistic and tradition-bound society is that worship is not encouraged or even thought of except within organized religion.

Although Wicca is very much a personal, spontaneous religion, it does have an authoritative book which is not, like the Bible, available to the public, but is passed on by an initiator to the initiate. The book is called the *Book of Shadows*, and it is only for witches. The initiate must copy it by hand for his or her own use. It is not a book of dogma and the description of seasonal rituals, for instance, is in skeletal form so that each person or group can create their own rituals. It is core material only and all new witches are asked to write a second volume – their own personal *Book of Shadows* – which will be the invocations, rituals and spells that they have discovered to be the most effective in their own spiritual journey.

Some of us may feel that using spells and reciting invocations to

Gods and Goddesses could never be appropriate in our own lives. Our rationality rebels. Vivianne, who is herself a very rational person, is well aware of this: 'Often when people become interested in Wicca, their thinking side protests that it cannot believe in elementals and magic, and that mighty Gods and Goddesses stalk the Earth. This does not matter and blind willingness to see everything as literal is as foolish as people believing that the Earth is flat.'

She tells us that Wicca operates in two realms of truth. One is metaphysical truth, such as our ancestors accepted, which said that if the correct rites were not observed at the Winter Solstice the sun would die. The other realm is psychological truth which tells us that if one dismisses such a concept altogether it is the inner sun of our spiritual world which dies.

What we need, she says, is a very simple belief that our consciousness is not dependent on the body but can extend beyond the limits of the sense world. In this way we feel reverence for the life-force. Other than such belief in the life-force and the powers of the human psyche, all that is needed is that we come to accept the framework of ritual and symbols in which Wicca operates, and accept it as containing age-old truths which are not literal but which are hidden and which will unfold to us over the years as we integrate them into our lives.

For Vivianne, as a trained psychologist, the work of Carl Jung has played an important role in her views of Wicca. She sees the evolving of a priest or priestess who is discovering (or recovering) the Self as similar to Jung's process of individuation. It is a process of becoming who and what we really are.

Becoming who we are is also bound up with our sexuality and Vivianne feels that the traditional suppression of women in religion has been because of negative attitudes to sex. For when woman is seen as seductress and temptress, men feel they must be protected from her by segregating her and keeping her apart, but this can only lead to the spiritual impoverishment of both sexes and thus of society. Many women have had to secretly develop themselves and their psychic powers and a lot of their knowledge and wisdom has been suppressed or lost – Vivianne calls this lost knowledge the Wise Craft. It is the knowledge of magic and of healing powers traditionally associated with witches. In other societies less fearful of sex and of the unknown, a witch would be called a Wise Woman or a priestess.

Witches believe that all human beings have innate powers to bring about change by using the mind properly and the energy fields of the body. They also believe that consciousness is free, not confined to the physical realm and the laws of time, but by its nature able to travel forwards and backwards and to glimpse the past and the future. Awareness of such freedom comes often in dream, but it can be developed with psychic training. Women are often thought to be especially gifted in this awareness and many women who have come to understand their own psyche and energy flows have discovered that they are able to develop such freedom and the power to travel through time.

In earlier societies, people were aware that women's cycles were accompanied by psychic and psychological change. Menstruating women were considered dangerous. Witches are aware that menstruating women have a high level of psychokinetic energy – the energy which causes poltergeist and other magical manifestations. At other times of the menstrual cycle, the psyche is more open to the dream world. Through attuning to their inner cycles and seasons, women become aware of their psychic tides and learn to know the times when big dreams will come, dreams which give messages which cut across the limitations of normal awareness.

It has not been easy for women to exercise the powers of Wise Craft in recent Western society. The use by women of magical powers has been strongly suppressed and condemned by the male Church. Even woman's traditional role as healer and midwife has been hijacked by a male medical establishment. However, the image of Witch, which is closely aligned to that of Shaman, offers women the possibility of harnessing this power and of using it in positive ways which benefit humankind – to heal and to change that which should be changed.

The images of woman as priestess and Witch are important and empowering to women. Recent societies have taught [and some societies still teach] that woman is passive, a womb to bear children, the field which awaits the plough, that which is to be impregnated and controlled by men and male society. The Goddess images in Western society have also taken on those images. The Virgin Mary of Christian religion is 'the handmaid of the Lord' and women's religious role has for centuries been that of follower and subordinate to the male priest. In Christianity women have been permitted to serve God as nuns, but only recently has women's entry to the priesthood been contemplated. In Paganism the image of the Goddess is of strength and power. Woman is honoured as priestess, Wise Woman and Woman of Power. Women are urged not to be passive vessels at the disposal of men, but women in control of their own destiny: 'Priestesses in their own right, strong and proud, with their own vision.'

Wiccans believe the body to be a gift from the Gods, the vessel of the divine Self, and so it must be treated with respect and care. It is particularly important that Wiccans do not lose touch with the earth, even if they live in cities, but make time to go to the country and immerse themselves in natural forces. 'If we take the time to walk upon the earth, expose ourselves to the sky and Sun, and absorb the energies of water and trees, their energies will replenish us . . .'

The initiation ceremony, therefore, will usually take place outside unless the weather forbids it. The first thing the initiate must do is take off his or her clothes, for the rites of Wicca are performed naked. This is to emphasize the disappearance of the normal everyday persona of the individual. It has another symbolic meaning too, which is that when naked we are very vulnerable.

By being willing to expose ourselves in a very literal sense, we have to make an act of love and trust, the two passwords which bring us into the circle, and we also have to be willing to cast aside our persona and enter the circle as we first entered the world, naked and vulnerable. It is as a child seeking entry into the world that we come to the edge of the circle for initiation.

We are born full of fears, fears of the unknown and of the dark, and these are fears of both what is within and what is without. We are afraid to look within ourselves because there is much about ourselves which we despise and of which we are ashamed and we do not wish to acknowledge this to ourselves, let alone to others, but in Wicca we must face these things; we must see our souls naked and unveiled. We are afraid of the dark, the 'things that go bump in the night', but we must enter that darkness. We must discover the forces that surround us and which move the universe. We must look upon the faces of the Goddess and the God.

A candidate for initiation is blindfolded and bound by three ritual cords. One cord is tied round the wrists, which are placed upright behind the back. That cord is then taken up and passed round the initiate's neck from where it goes back loosely to the wrists again and then once more up to the neck, leaving a long loose end at the front by which the blindfold initiate can be led. Another cord is tied around the initiates left knee and the last round the right ankle, so that the initiate's feet are 'neither bound nor free'. Thus he or she is not quite committed yet and can draw back at the last moment.

This binding, Vivianne tells us, symbolizes the spiritual state before the initiation and the cords are known as 'the material basis'. Before the rite the initiate is still a prisoner of the world, bound by materialism and the demands of the ego – and yet not completely. By seeking initiation the first step on the path of a spiritual journey has been taken and the feet are already nearly free. At the end of the initiation the cords are removed and the fetters which hold the spirit back from its destiny can be thrown away: 'We are set free to seek and find ourselves.'

Immediately before the ceremony, the initiate is given two pass-words – Perfect Love and Perfect Trust. Perfect Love, it is believed, becomes possible within the circle of initiates because of the trust in the divine archetypes. 'If we invoke the Great Mother and the Sky Father, archetypes of female and male love, our egos will absorb the qualities of those archetypes and it is possible to manifest them in our own lives.'

The coven is the community of witches and it is also the commun-ity of the Goddess and the God. It is to be entered as home, a place where wholeness, truth and love can grow to spiritual maturity. Enter-ing a circle with somebody else is thought to be one of the most intimate things one can do with another person. And with the re-moval of the clothes goes the removal of all sorts of other barriers to intimacy. The friendships formed within the new spiritual family, the coven, bring into being very strong bonds between people and this is looked upon as one of the pleasures of coven life.

After the initiate has been taken through the many rituals and has been received into the coven, he or she learns how to make magic. A change of consciousness is needed and this is often helped by chanting while taking part in a circle dance. Dancing has always been a part of tribal and group worship – records of a circle dance remain in the fossilized footprints of Paleolithic people thirty thousand years ago. The object of the dance might then have been to communicate with animals by shamanic means. In later Dionysian and Roman times it included group sexual activity. In Wicca today the dance is to achieve a unity of the mind rather than the body, for the rhythmical movement of the dance helps the dancers to release the hold of the ego and to allow individual minds to merge into a group entity. Traditional witches have always believed that the human body has a latent power within it which can be released through various ways, particularly dancing. It is known as etheric energy or power and Vivianne tells us that learning to release this force is a matter of practice like learning to drive a car. Once released, this etheric power must be harnessed and put to use, though: 'In making magic we must scrupulously examine our motives for each piece of work we do, and if we are asked for magical help we must use our wisdom to decide whether it is truly beneficial for the person concerned . . .'

The way of using the etheric energy raised by the dance is to enter a changed state of consciousness where the psyche of the witch and of the person needing help begin to merge. As they merge, and the witch enters the psychic space of the one to be healed, the witch can visualize the healing needed and implant it into the psyche of the other.

To Vivianne all such practices are reminders of our interconnectedness, our oneness of being. As she discovered when she was a small child, there is no separateness in nature. 'Everything, both animate and inanimate, is interconnected. Every apparently separate thing, whether a rock or stone, animal, plant, human or event, is linked. All things are part of a greater whole and therefore in communication with one another. The apparent separateness of things is an illusion.'

So, if all things are interconnected, then by examining any one part of the extraordinary world we can gain insights into the whole.

To Vivianne the whole is the Self, the wiser and deeper part of ourselves.

To find the Self . . . we must make a spiritual journey. This is the process of spiritual initiation. The initiation ceremonies which make us an adult member of society, or which initiate us into a particular religious tradition, are entry points to this process, but they are not the process itself. The process is life-long – hence the sight of the Grail often ends in death; for after we have achieved total Oneness with the ultimate reality, then we have reached our spiritual home. No more journeying forth is necessary.

Ma Yoga Shakti

'We are all the children of one infinite source. But we overlook our source and borrow identities from religion, from culture, from language, from our land and people, and then we get stuck with that identity. As long as we need it, we will love it. But when we grow out of it, then we can make our own decisions and explore where we want because this whole universe is God.'

The title Ma Yoga Shakti means Mother of the Inner Power of Yoga but her many Indian, European and American followers use the more affectionate name of Mataji – Honoured Mother. Mataji was born into a wealthy Hindu family in Varanasi (Benares) in 1927. As a girl, she did not merit much status in Hindu society, a fact which gave her a feminist viewpoint from an early age. But fortunately her family was a loving one, her father a wise and liberal man with friends of all religions, and she was able to develop into an independent-thinking young woman. She went to university and took a degree in political science, and with all the vigour of her youth battled to change Indian society, particularly in its attitude to women.

She married when she was eighteen – she is a strong believer in marriage and advises all people to marry before they begin their spiritual life – and started a family. But when her four children were growing up she felt free to go back to an academic life. She became the founder and also the principal of a college for young women in Bihar. Part of the college was also a school for girls and soon Mataji was very active indeed. She had strong views on women's education, believing they should develop their own lives and become as free as possible in the caste-ridden and restricted society of the fifties.

Inevitably such a stance led her into politics and she was persuaded to stand for Congress. But a woman candidate was unlikely to win at that time and although she lost by only some two hundred votes, she felt that this door would remain closed to her. At the same time too, she had the strong sensation that she was being called to other work. When she was younger she had been fascinated by the gods and goddesses of Hindu religion and the high ideals they represented. Like the different rays of the sun, each was an aspect of the one God, their source. As a child she had often felt herself in touch with divinity and a greater consciousness had seemed very close to her. She longed to know the unknown and to be part of a spiritual world that she felt was present all the time if she could but reach it.

Varanasi, the holy city of India, was at one time the base of Annie Besant, President of the Theosophical Society, and to this day the centre she founded, surrounded by its beautiful gardens, lies like a secret island of peace in the middle of the turbulent town. Mataji was to find in the life of Annie Besant a source of inspiration that she never lost. By the time Mataji became aware of her, Annie was dead, but her life and personality affected Mataji strongly. For Annie too had been a social reformer before she became a Theosophist and Mataji could see strong parallels between their lives.

Like Mataji, Annie had married young and had borne children before she felt an urge to put right certain things in society. Unlike Mataji though, Annie, who was married to a vicar, had had the formidable Victorian Church of England with all its entrenched respectability to contend with, and after she left her husband and declared herself an atheist she was made to suffer for breaking all society's rules by losing her children, which was a desperate grief to her. But as a Socialist and anti-Church reformer, she put her energy into writing pamphlets and lecturing up and down the country. She fought for greater freedom and justice in almost every area – marriage, birth control, working conditions, the law, motherhood, poverty, education and politics. She was a brilliant speaker and made history with the changes she brought about in the status of women and the poor. Some of her reforms have lasted to this day, such as the introduction of school meals and reform of factory law.

Unknown to most people though, throughout all her formidable battles, she had been haunted by a sense of loss. She had rejected Christianity but was essentially a spiritual person and still looked for answers to what she called 'the riddle of life and mind'. What are we here for? Why do people have to suffer? These were the questions that Mataji too was asking: 'What is the divine and what is the self? Is this earthly life an experiment in consciousness?'

Annie had thought that Socialism was the solution to all problems but she began to feel that political and economic answers were not enough. She felt that there was 'some hidden thing, some hidden power' which would transform life if she could find it. And in her early forties, she believed she had. She met Helena Blavatsky, the leader of the Theosophical Society, and it changed her life. The beliefs that Blavatsky put forward were very popular at the time and still retain a large following. They were the ideas that Mataji, in her time, was to be transformed by. The word theosophy itself means 'divine wisdom' and Mataji, like Annie before her, longed to know more of such wisdom: 'The world seemed full of differences and varieties,' she says. 'These could be considered as beautiful, creative expressions of mankind and the differences make the world very interesting. But I realized that these differences in people's lives and outlooks and above all in their religions meant that the whole vision of the divine was not yet seen and only a partial truth revealed.'

The Theosophical Society was founded in 1875 and in 1878 the headquarters moved to India because its main beliefs were derived from Hinduism and Buddhism. Indeed, it was Blavatsky who opened up the world of Eastern religion to the West. When Annie Besant became the leader of the Society in her mid-forties, she went to India and found it to be her true spiritual home. She spent most of the rest of her life there, loving the country and its people deeply. She founded schools and colleges and encouraged the study of Indian philosophy, arts and religion because she believed this was the way to revive the greatness of India. She campaigned for better rights for Indian women and she fought fiercely for self-government, believing the British should leave the country. In 1917 the British interned her as a troublemaker but although she was by then nearly seventy nothing could keep her down. The protest at her internment was so strong that the British government was forced to let her free and she was then elected President of the Indian National Congress. The fact that India should elect a woman, and a British one, to be their President showed the admiration they had for her.

So it was quite natural that Annie Besant was the torch to fire Mataji's imagination, for in that great woman she could see a reflection of herself. She could see her own determination to reform the position of women in Indian society and her own desire to educate women through her college and school. Living in the same town as

Annie had, she felt an intimate kinship with that amazing woman whose life had coincided with her own for her first six years (Annie died in 1933).

But, above all, it was Annie's spiritual transformation that touched Mataji the most deeply. She herself had spent some years in politics and outward reforms, but now the sense of something greater to discover was with her all the time, as it was with Annie when she first encountered the Theosophical Society. And, as Annie had done, Mataji too began to feel that Theosophy was her path. She founded a Theosophical Lodge in Annie Besant's name and says: 'Theosophy became to me the most important thing in my life.'

From a very young age she had been conscious of 'beings' or 'influences' that she could not see with her eyes but that were somehow there, waiting to be contacted. Such feelings were now revived and endorsed by Theosophy, which believes that evolution is manifold and that humanity fills a comparatively small place in nature. 'It becomes clear to the student,' says C W Leadbeater, a founder, whose book inspired Mataji, 'that just as earth, air and water support myriads of forms of life which, though invisible to the ordinary eye, are revealed to us by the microscope, so the higher planes connected with our earth have an equally dense population of whose existence we are ordinarily completely unconscious.'

These higher planes are attainable by us, Theosophists believe, through rebirth; for people are part of a cycle of life in which each existence brings one nearer to a more exalted spiritual level. Theosophy teaches that there is a higher self in each of us which we should nurture throughout successive reincarnations until we are liberated from the flesh. It is thought that the universe is composed of seven planes of existence. Watching over the whole process are Mahatmas, or Masters. In their astral bodies they visit select disciples to convey their message to the world.

It was the astral plane that Mataji herself felt very close to. Although Theosophy teaches that the astral is but one of many levels of consciousness, it is regarded as the nearest 'heavenly' one to humans and the most easily accessible. It is the next 'above' the physical world. To the Theosophical student the astral world is totally real. As Leadbeater says: 'The objects and inhabitants of the astral plane are real in exactly the same way as our own bodies, our furniture, our houses and monuments are real. They will no more endure for ever than will objects on the physical plane, but they are nevertheless realities from our point of view while they last – realities which we cannot afford to ignore merely because the majority of mankind is as yet unconscious, or but vaguely conscious, of their existence.'

Theosophists believe that each plane of being has a different degree of density and our physical plane is the most dense. It is possible to be in touch with some of the other planes, particularly the astral, and, as Leadbeater tells us, the first introduction comes to people in various ways: 'Some, only once in their whole lives under some unusual influence, become sensitive enough to recognize the presence of one of its inhabitants; others find themselves with increasing frequency seeing and hearing something to which those around them are blind and deaf; others again – and perhaps this is the commonest experience of all – begin to recollect with greater and greater clearness that which they have seen or heard on that other plane during sleep. But, however it may occur, the first actual realization that we are all the while in the midst of a great world full of active life, of which most of us are nevertheless entirely unconscious, cannot but be to some extent a memorable epoch in a man's existence.'

Many people have had the experience of feeling some other presence in the atmosphere. Rudolf Steiner, for instance, was convinced that he had a 'clairvoyant perception' when he was a child and could see Beings around him. He always said that what he saw were facts about life that other people did not see and there are undoubtedly many people who would know exactly what he meant. He took the view, similar to the Theosophical view, that each quality – love, goodness, mercy – has its pure original in a world beyond the limitations of the human mind. Steiner saw these pure originals as actual Beings radiating their qualities to earth, of which we catch the shadow as they become concepts in our mind.

Mataji too had always been aware of such luminous presences in her own life and when she first read Leadbeater's book on the astral plane she felt that she had discovered a kindred soul. She was led to the Theosophical Society, to Annie Besant, and to a whole new world of understanding. Theosophy changed her life. She says:

'From my own personal experiences, I feel that there are great psychic beings who can be close at hand to help if we turn our minds towards them.'

Mataji believes that each child is a perfect soul, trapped in the body for some divine reason beyond human understanding: 'While we live in this world, our better part is within, and receives very little attention. By the time we reach adulthood, the pressure of family and society has grown to such an extent that the inner being is lacking the proper food needed to improve its sphere of awareness.'

She herself, she tells us, found that the Indian god Hanuman provided this nourishment for her:

Thoughts create, as well as travel. Thought-forms have power. By thinking and feeling intensely we create an astral entity which is as real and true as anything in the outside world. Such an angelic form belongs to the astral world, which cannot be approached through the five sense organs. Hanuman is the one who has been an eternal companion, friend, guide, protector and saviour to me. I have tried to reach Him in my own mind, whenever it was needed. He has always been accessible in my mind, just as one carries a pocket calculator or a reference book. I am mentally committed to Him. I have drawn my inspiration from His life and deeds, and it doesn't matter to me whether His existence is a historical fact or not.

The human mind loves myths and unrealities. When I speak of Hanuman, I am reminded of the stories about Him, which are the means of gaining insight into the layers of time. According to Indian mythology there have been repetitions of many ages, like pages in a book. Hanuman was born in one of the chapters of the present age and is said to be blessed with eternal life. He is a symbol of the human mind and the way the mind can become virtuous by calling upon virtue.

The mind has to be shown the way. If the mind sees, hears, smells or touches something, then it is helped to grow. It needs a model to shape itself in some particular direction. Hundreds of myths and characters were developed in India through intuitive knowledge, meditation and rituals, to set a goal for the human mind to attain. It seems that the wise people of old tried to weave a pattern of mythological and mystical realities to raise human consciousness. People in India build up their psychic faith and employ it for their welfare. Psychic faith is beyond reasoning. It is more powerful than the intellect. It is like an inner chord and when it is touched things happen without any effort. Psychic laws can do things for you when you have faith.

Many people call on Hanuman and he is famous for several characteristics, such as bravery. By reading the story of Hanuman, or by chanting prayers to Him, or by praising His virtues, or by trying to invoke His presence – we invoke the hidden powers of our own mind. By believing in Him we learn to believe in our own souls. The ultimate reality is a very mysterious one; by raising one's consciousness to the highest point, one becomes one with God. Saint Tulsidas has rightly expressed this: 'By knowing You one becomes like You.'

When we learn devotion we become one with God. There is only one way to reach God, 'give yourself up'. Without giving or losing ourselves we can never reach God. All the mythical characters created by the powerful vision of the sages have become real identities in the psychic world. Characters like Hanuman, Ganesh, Angels and others have become true entities of a different world, with which we are constantly communicating through the smooth flow of our consciousness.

Devotion to Hanuman means seeing Him as a symbol of courage, fearlessness and energy. One who prays to Hanuman is always freed from fear and problems. By chanting prayers to Him again and again, one promotes his psychic energy and strengthens his relationship with the psychic world.

Those of us in the West who were brought up as Christians may see many similarities between Mataji's attitude to Hanuman and a simple Christian attitude to Christ. There is the same belief in his universality and also in his actual presence, in his role as comforter and his power to dissolve fear. He can be approached through prayer, talked to, confided in, yet he does not live on the same plane as ourselves. The need to believe in such a mythological person, whether Indian god or disembodied Christ, angel or genie, seems a powerful part of the human psyche.

And yet it would be wrong to deny that invisible beings exist, even if many of us never experience them or feel a need for them. They are real for those who want them. Mataji says, 'Psychic levels are there. If you take any divine representative and if you are honest and truthful, it will help you always. There are millions of people on this earth and there may be many hundreds of ways or rays of reality, just as the sun has many rays. One sun shines on all the countries. As long as we have one sun and one moon, we are all one family.'

For those of us who still have reservations about calling on psychic beings, there may be another way of regarding the astral plane. In near-death experiences, many have reported travelling down a long tunnel towards a bright light which envelops them with feelings of love and warmth and joy. Some also report an encounter with a Being of Light and this has often led to a belief in God as a result. Although the experiencer feels it 'realer than here, really', the encounter with the Being does not mean that it has an objective reality or lives in a place that can be discovered. The Being's reality is entirely in the mind of the experiencer under the special conditions operating at the point of death, and those conditions are appropriate to whatever that person has encountered and understood during his or her life.

The tunnel and the light are now considered to be the physiological effects of the brain as it dies, but the Being can be seen in another way. Something is there, but what it is is a mystery, and each of us as we approach it find our own reality in it. For instance, A J Ayer, who was a celebrated atheist, underwent strange and quite elaborate experiences of a red light and two creatures in charge of space, when his heart stopped beating for four minutes during a bout of pneumonia. When he awoke from the sleep which followed his return to life, he said to a friend beside his bed, 'Did you know that I was dead? The first time that I tried to cross the river I was frustrated, but my second attempt succeeded. It was most extraordinary, my thoughts became persons.'

'My thoughts became persons' is perhaps what most people experience when they temporarily 'die'. This does not invalidate the 'Being' that many see. We each create a transcendental environment according to where our thoughts and beliefs in life have led us and the Being is no less 'real' than anything else that has happened to us. As Danah Zohar has shown, we can never know reality directly, it always has to come to us filtered by our mind. So there is something awaiting us at the point of death but what that is is a mystery. It seems as though the sense of a spiritual life with which each one of us is endowed manifests uniquely at the point of death – but the manifestation itself is not the same for everybody. It is revealed according to the way each mind operates. For, as Iris Murdoch has pointed out, the innate feeling of a spiritual life is the reality of which God is the imaginative construct. Rather than a universal deity awaiting everybody at death, is it not more likely that each of us will find the exact manifestation we need to help us through that change of existence?

If we can accept that there is a spiritual dimension which manifests to each of us according to our needs, then there can be no reason to deny another's discoveries simply because they do not accord with our own. As Danah Zohar points out, our differences are the expressed potentialities of a common source; and the otherness of the other, those very differences, are essential for our own growth and understanding. Therefore another's reality is not to be questioned, but to be encountered with interest and attention.

It is in this way that those of us who have not experienced the astral plane can learn something about these other forms of existence which a number of people seem to have discovered. Mataji certainly was inspired by such a form when, at the age of twenty-two, she became aware that one of the great and invisible Masters the Theosophists believe in had visited her in her spirit.

A great invisible saint, whose medium I am, lived many years ago and it was He who gave me His vision as a guiding spirit in the early part of my life. His name in the unseen world is 'Morya Deva'. Out of love and reverence I call Him 'Master M'. In 1949 I became aware of the task commissioned to me by the master. I cannot see Him directly but I can always feel His presence and power behind me.

During my early life, my mind became fascinated by higher ideals and the transformation of my subconscious personality slowly set in. Thereafter I used to feel the presence of my master in my thoughts, words and deeds. My mission in this world is to do my best for Master M.

Believe in the existence of an invisible and unseen world. There are many worlds beyond, invisible to human sight, and inaccessible to human knowledge. You have come from that realm and you will return to the same place. Many perfected and divine beings exist in those worlds. Their co-operation, grace and blessings are boons to mankind.

If you have sincere desire, devotion and loving feelings in your mind for these invisible saints and angels, you will be able to experience their presence and grace. You may see their manifestation or receive their guidance in your dreams and meditation.

Human beings have to learn to expand their consciousness. They are born to become divine. It is to help people to grow out of their restrictions, their borrowed identities, that I teach understanding of the body and of the self. If people ask 'What am I?' they begin to explore and find new insight.

To be of service to humankind was Mataji's growing aim and thus it was that she worked for her women's college at the same time as she tried to become aware of the Divine within her life and of what she was being truly asked to do. In this, once more, she resembled Annie Besant and, like that other reformer who dropped everything to begin a spiritual life, so Mataji, at the age of forty-four, ended her whole family and social life and left her home to enter the holy order of Sanyasa. She became a sanyasi – one who has no past or possessions and lives only to perform the works of God: 'My religion became Truth,' she said, 'and I was no longer tied by any other form of religion.'

Within a very few years Mataji had become a widely respected teacher of yoga and her wisdom, dignity, motherly nature and broad-mindedness began to attract many people. She was regarded as a guru and her ashram became crowded with followers anxious to draw on her spiritual understanding.

Every three years there is a gathering of teachers in India, called the Kumbha Mela. Honours are conferred and gurus recognized. In 1969 Mataji was given the title of saint and in 1975 a further title was added, that of Maha – great teacher.

Yet such classifications are put in the background when one actually talks to Mataji, for she is delightfully informal and at one with her questioner. She is prepared to do anything – sit and talk or provide a meal or go for a walk. In India people kiss her feet but she has no expectations of this in the West and is faintly reproving when somebody will stoop to do so in a public place. She is thoroughly down to earth and accepting of whatever she finds and this makes for an unselfconscious and true encounter. Mataji is small and she sweeps along in her golden sari with energy and force. Her face is full of character and it is impossible to think of her as anything but independent. She is still a feminist and regrets the universal belief that God is masculine, and she still, at the age of sixty-nine, is determined to save the world through her teaching of yoga.

'My teaching is yoga, of the mind and of the body. The body is not just flesh; everything is hidden in the shell of the body. Yoga helps to balance body and mind, the two wings of the bird which is the soul. It is a discipline and people must learn to discipline themselves for they cannot expect everything from others.

'Most people come to spiritual practice because they are unhappy, and that I don't like. When you are happy – *then* practise! But yoga helps the unhappy by showing them how to see into their own mind and to enrich it until thoughts and emotions are under better control. You should think consciously and not out of impulse or habit or addiction or borrowed philosophies. You should try to have good thoughts – the effect may not be noticed but the vibrations clean up the air nevertheless.'

The word yoga has the same root as our word yoke and it means to join or unite. In Hinduism it is a way of spiritual union, a practical discipline to bring the follower to oneness with God. In the West yoga is usually thought of as a system of bodily postures for health and well-being, which is Hatha Yoga, and certainly this is one of the aspects that Mataji emphasizes for she feels that it is through the body that many people come to realization But there are other forms of yoga and Indians have always recognized that people are not alike and the way that suits one may not suit another. Thus there are four main yogas for four general kinds of people: those who are active; those who are thoughtful and contemplative; those who have a loving heart and find devotion the way; and those of an inquiring and intellectual disposition, who want to study and discover the workings of the mind. Mataji teaches all forms.

Karma yoga, for instance, is learning to serve in a selfless way. It means a real surrender of oneself to God, for then one acts in the consciousness that God is the doer, God is the thinker and God is the feeler. It is accepting that everything, even one's body and mind, are 'on loan' and that the life that lives one is vastly greater than oneself and the breath that breathes one is never for a moment one's own. Karma yoga is the yoga of selfless action, an uninvolved service to whatever situation life puts in front of one without expectation of result.

Jnana yoga is knowledge, but it is the understanding and clarifying of wisdom as distinct from ordinary information that is its essence. A Jnana student seeks to discover his or her essential being when all the descriptions of it such as name, age and position in the world have been dropped. To quote the Indian sage Ramana Maharshi: 'Under whatever name and form one may worship the Absolute Reality, it is only a means for realizing it without name and form. That alone is true realization, wherein one knows oneself in relation to that reality, attains peace and realizes one's identity with it.' Jnana Yoga is thus a yoga of contemplation.

Bhakti Yoga is the path of devotion and surrender to God. It is adoration and worship and many people world-wide find this an easier path than the intellectual or contemplative. But Hindu psychology recognizes that there are different ways of loving and Bhakti is not a simple sentimentality for it involves learning at least five ways to develop a devotion to God which will mature at every step. This is the yoga of prayer, ritual and ceremony.

Finally Raja Yoga, which is the path of insight. Essentially it is the yoga of psychology for it uses personal experience as its basis. Raja Yoga states that the external world is a gross form of the subtle, or internal, world of the mind. The external is the effect and the internal is the cause. Thus, by learning to manipulate the internal forces, the yogi will gain remarkable expression of his powers; he will gain control of the manifested world and pass beyond the point where the laws of nature have any influence on him. He accomplishes this difficult journey first by way of mastering the body through the *asanas* of Hatha Yoga and then through the control of breathing; this leads to the control of the mind through concentration.

Mataji teaches all these aspects of yoga. She believes that people benefit immeasurably from learning them. She follows a treatise of yoga written by a medieval yogi, Gherand Samita, which she has translated; and in her books she gives her own helpful commentary, including an occult explanation, as an accompaniment to his directions. 'I teach yoga because it is a good tool,' she tells us. 'Through yoga I can give a message to people. The branches of yoga cover all aspects of life and by practising yoga you are able to explore every level.'

If yoga can be said to have a goal beyond the integration of body, mind and spirit it is the state called samadhi. 'Samadhi means,' says Mataji, 'merging the mind into Absolute Consciousness, or uniting the mind with the Supreme Cosmic Consciousness. In this state one attains sublime equanimity. When the mind comes back to physical consciousness after samadhi, it is full of vigour, knowledge and wisdom.'

Samadhi is not attained easily, she tells us, and cannot be brought about without the help of a guru. However there are some techniques which she is willing to share with anyone who reads her books. One is Shambhavi Mudra, a visualization. You should meditate on your own inner self as though seated in the middle of the sky, she tells us. 'Now meditate as if the sky were within you as well as outside. See yourself as fully wrapped with the sky all around and within you. You should feel the sky above you, beneath you, inside you and all around you. You feel yourself as a small bird flying far in the sky for an endless time. Thus live and experience the eternal bliss, and enter into samadhi.'

Another technique is to use an internal sound. You inhale air slowly and hold it within yourself. Putting your fingers in your ears, you then listen to the inner sound, which is said to resemble a bee's hum. 'Even a newborn baby,' says Mataji, 'is very sensitive to sound vibrations. Children like sounds and similarly the minds of adults are easily captivated by sound. It is a very pleasant and self-absorbing practice to listen to the sound which is eternally echoing within ourselves. If you close your ears and stop the outer sound vibrations from entering, you will listen to a melodious sound constantly humming in your ears.'

Mataji also teaches the understanding and use of the chakras, the seven psychic centres of the body. This teaching is used in the next technique, in which you should meditate on your chosen deity in the region of your heart chakra. You should give your full devotion, love and joy to this meditation until you are carried away by the depth of your emotion, your body shivering with adoration (some of this technique is perhaps used today by Christian Charismatics). To a reserved Westerner, this may sound a bit overwhelming, but Mataji believes strongly in the merits of emotion when it is rightly directed and is convinced we don't allow ourselves enough of it.

'Emotions are good if they are not wasted on trifling matters. Emotion is a great force and can work wonders providing one knows how to use it properly. Humans are by nature emotional. But we waste our emotional energy on trifling habits and feelings whereas if the emotion is directed for good, it can bring permanent results to the world. Emotion directed truly can lead to samadhi.

'Samadhi itself is a word which is most fascinating and most abstruse. Some are very attracted by it, while others are sceptical about it. In fact, samadhi is a science of the mind which has many dimensions. So far psychologists have seen only three dimensions of the mind, namely the conscious, the subconscious and the unconscious. But in yoga it is believed that a person has seven phases of his consciousness. In samadhi all these phases are explored.

'But even so, this is still a tool, a technique for reaching something else. There is something – call it Mother, Father, Nature, God – whatever you like, but it is a great void, a Nothingness. Compared to our human consciousness, it is void. In the same way that the sun is burning at a high degree so our consciousness on that scale is a very few degrees. We live life as though it is a dream – and we might as well dream it well! – but behind it is the Nothingness, a reality which the five senses and the mind cannot grasp. But our mind is a function of that reality, of that Void.'

But it is too difficult for humans to live with the concept of that Nothingness, Mataji believes, and thus we need gods or a God on which to focus our spiritual feelings. 'Very often we project our human feelings onto God and think he is as we are. And if you want God on that level or on any other level of consciousness, you will find him. Focus your attention, open any window of any design and the light of the Void will come through. And the design is not very important. One person may prefer one more than the others, but all are openings. I think if we could stop trying to convert people to our own design, it would be a very good thing. In my ashrams I have many windows – images of Christ, the Buddha and all the religions, as well as Ram, Ganesh and others.'

Mataji has ashrams in India, New York and Florida and she is hoping to start one in England. She regards her ashrams as family homes where her 'family' of followers can be together. She herself, as a sanyasi, does not live in any one of them but comes and goes.

'To me, the world is God's guesthouse and I am living as a guest here. It is a beautiful place. But I believe there is much more – many universes – and where God will send me next I don't know.'

Jung Chang

'He had been part of my life ever since I was a child. He was the idol, the god, the inspiration. The purpose of my life had been formulated in his name. A couple of years before, I would happily have died for him. Although his magic power had vanished from inside me, he was still sacred and undoubtable.'

In these lines Jung Chang is not talking of Jesus or the Buddha but of Chairman Mao. For she is a daughter of Communist China and her remarkable life, revealed in her book *The Wild Swans*, has given us – in a way that perhaps no other book has ever done – a deep insight into the religion of ideology.

Jung Chang was born in 1952 in Chengdu, a town in Sichuan Province, where she was to spend most of her early life. At her birth she was called Er-hong, meaning second Wild Swan. Her mother, the first Wild Swan, had come from a strange and romantic background, for her mother had been the concubine of a famous general and she herself was the child of this general. But when she was still a baby, her mother, the concubine, had been forced to escape with her child from the general's mansion where she was kept a prisoner, for the general was dying and as his concubine she would almost certainly be sent to a brothel by his wife and thus lose her baby. In spite of her bound feet, which made every step agony, she managed to escape and to take the baby to Yixian, two hundred miles away, where she felt safe. An old schoolfriend arranged shelter for her in the house of her father-in-law, a kindly old doctor, Dr Xia, who eventually fell in love with her and married her, adopting her daughter as his own child. It was then that he gave the little girl, Jung Chang's mother, the new name of De-hong, Wild Swan. When De-hong herself later had a daughter, Jung Chang's elder sister, the baby was called Xia-hong, a Wild Swan like her mother, and when Jung Chang was born, the doctor said: 'Ah, another Wild Swan' and Er-hong was her name until, aged thirteen, she asked to change it to something more military, for it had the same pronunciation as 'faded red' which the schoolchildren had been warned the country might become unless they were all loyal Communists. Her father gave her the name Jung, meaning martial affairs.

Jung's grandmother, the concubine, was to play a major part in her life, for when the old doctor died she came to live with the family and was a constant support for the children when their parents were away, as they often were. She read them stories, both Chinese and foreign, and chanted classical poems to them. She came from a rich background, had been highly educated, and was elegant and accomplished in many ways, as well as very tranquil and loving. She was a Buddhist and meditated every day to give herself objectivity of mind. Such a quality came to be essential for the growing family as both Jung's parents held responsible positions in the Communist Party and were frequently absent. Her father was a high Party official and her mother was head of the Youth League in the town. Jung's father in particular believed totally in Communist ideals – his childhood had been a deprived and unhappy one under the old privileged regime of Chiang Kai-shek and also under the Japanese invasion of China. So for him Communism was the beginning of a brave new world. But Jung's mother, who had also suffered under the Japanese and who welcomed Communism to begin with, was nevertheless often appalled by its barbarous acts, such as the execution of a friend, a young colonel in the Kuomintang, the old regime. Indeed, it was this execution which came eventually to affect the whole family, for when Jung was three her mother was taken into detention while her name was cleared of association with him.

She was away for six months, but in the end was told she could go back to work as long as she reported every evening. She realized that the investigations must have bogged down through lack of evidence and the suspicions could not be proved or disproved. As soon as she was free, she rushed to see her children in their different nurseries. Jung remembers the evening she came to see her. She was nearly four, and was in a wooden bed with railings. One side was let down so that her mother could sit and hold her hand while she fell asleep. But Jung longed to tell her about all her adventures and was worried that once she fell asleep her mother would disappear again forever. Whenever her mother tried to slip her hand away, she gripped it and began to cry. Her mother stayed until around midnight and Jung screamed when she started to leave, but she had to pull herself away for her 'parole' time was up.

Thus began Jung's life of insecurity. She was never to know, throughout her childhood, if her mother or father would be allowed to remain at home (although after eighteen months of great anxiety, her mother was officially cleared), for as the years went by Mao launched one witch-hunt after another and the number of victims rose, each victim bringing down many others. Because of this iron control China was indeed stable for some years – the old terrors of foreign invasion, death from starvation, bandits and so on seemed in the past. 'Stability, the dream of the Chinese, sustained the faith of people like my mother in their suffering,' says Jung. And at least her grandmother was there; she had arrived to take all the children out of their nurseries and bring them home.

Jung's mother trod a tense high-wire line with the Party because she knew within herself that she had doubts about the system, although for the sake of her family she must never utter such doubts. But Jung's father never doubted and it is through this idealistic, righteous man of immense integrity, but also some rigidity, that we are shown the nature of Communism as a religion – a religion which Jung herself was to imbibe and believe implicitly

Professor Ninian Smart in *Religion and Nationalism* points out that nationalism commands in the modern world all the attributes of religion – its myths, its rituals, its ethos, its emotional force, its organization, its material manifestations and doctrines. It is true that it doesn't have a transcendental focus, like a God. But even here it may conceive itself as under the leadership of a God – and in China Mao certainly reached that elevation for many. All Professor Smart's classifications of religion can be seen in China: in the mythic dimension of the Party which acquired a power far greater than its individual section; in the rituals of celebrations and parades and marches where thousands acted as one; in the ethical dimension of becoming a good citizen and of living for the sake of the country rather than for oneself (this was carried to enormous lengths in China where every aspect of personal behaviour was scrutinized for imperfections or lack of loyalty); in the emotional force of belonging to a great movement, of being an appointed instrument of change; in the organization, political and hierarchical, which relied on reports and spying, and saying who is 'good' and who is 'bad' (every western religious parish takes part in this at some level); in the material manifestations of structures (such as churches or, as in the case of China, state buildings); and in the doctrinal dimension of the religion itself (in the case of Marxism, its ideals of common ownership and a land governed by the people, which came to be expressed so terribly in rules and imprisonments and the suppression of individual thinking).

Jung's father was a total believer in the Marxist ideal. Thus, although he loved his family, he always put the Party first and seemed to his children a hard man. It was only during the years of the Cultural Revolution that Jung saw him sometimes shocked and bewildered by the appalling outrages of the young Red Guards. He himself was in detention later on and towards the end of his life he lost his reason. Jung has an interesting theory about this, one which she did not put into *The Wild Swans*, but one which perhaps explains the strain from which 'believers' suffer, whether it is a religious or an ideological belief.

'My father was a very true person – or at least he tried to be. He was someone who was not happy to live with a compromise. He always wanted to be as true to himself as possible. And that's very difficult, of course, and it made him very difficult to live with. It's like living with a perfectionist and a puritan all the time. But he had to make compromises, he was forced to. Being in the Communist Party for so long, there were terrible things happening when he was there and he could not ignore them.

'He became disillusioned eventually but before that took place he had to undergo a lot of compromises. I feel that the more he tried to be true to himself, the more he undermined his integrity. I remember a friend, a scientist, who was the same – always trying to be true to himself. But every day there were political indoctrination sessions and you had to talk, everybody had to talk, had to say aloud that they gave their support. So he told me that his principle was that if he couldn't speak the truth at least he would not tell a lie. And that was very well said. But I was very irritated with him because I knew, and I think he knew, that it was impossible. For me, if I had to say at those meetings, for example, how wonderful Socialist China was – everybody had to say that because if you didn't you would immediately be victimized and get into horrible trouble – I knew I had to lie. In a way, I could tell the lie and be at peace with myself although I knew it was a lie. But for him – because he had this principle of not telling a lie and because he had to say Socialist China was wonderful, was Paradise, and because he knew that if you openly told the truth and defied the regime, not only you yourself got into trouble but your family, your friends, your relatives, your children – for him the consequences were too horrendous for him to make a principled stand and the whole moral equation was changed. So what happened to him, I noticed, was that he consciously made himself think Socialist China *was* wonderful and so in this way he could tell the truth. He brainwashed himself.'

Perhaps this observation sheds a light on many strange convictions that people hold, particularly in the more extreme religious sects, where enormous pressure is put on individuals to conform to a particular form of conduct or way of life. In some ways China could be compared to the Middle Ages in Europe when the torturers of the Catholic Inquisition forced neighbours to spy on and testify against each other, to make public confessions and to declare their fidelity to Catholicism. In very recent times the McCarthy witch-hunts in America had something of the same effect. A great deal of personal brainwashing must have gone on in the past and must surely still do so today whenever repressive techniques are used.

Jung is convinced that this brainwashing was at the root of her father's eventual breakdown, from which he luckily recovered before he died.

'If you openly defied the regime the consequences were too horrible, so you couldn't do it unless it was absolutely necessary. I think my father did renounce it during the Cultural Revolution, because the Cultural Revolution was so appalling with its violence and atrocities and he couldn't live with it all. So that overrode his considerations for his family and for his relatives. Before that, he had to put up with compromises and he had to tell himself that that was what he believed. So, in a way, his belief in Communism – I don't know how strong and genuine it really was without all the pressure. Once you joined the Chinese Communist Party you couldn't quit. To try to leave was regarded as to desert and you would be treated as a deserter, and you and your family would get into horrible trouble. So with all this pressure, I don't know how many people – my father included – really believed in Communism and were completely and spontaneously genuine. I think he told himself he believed because otherwise how could he live with that situation? To be consciously living a lie is difficult.

'My mother was quite different. I think, in a way, she was disillusioned ever since she came into contact with real Communism. I think when she was a young girl in the city, like so many other people, they projected on to this abstract idea of Communism their personal longings, their personal dreams. For my mother it was women's liberation – no more concubines, equality with men, and freedom and so on. There was always some personal dream for everybody and somehow it was all put into the idea of Communism. Many older people are now writing their memoirs of how they first came into contact with Communism and I think for many it was anguish. There came a period when they had to adjust to the reality of Communism but of course by then it was too late.

'So my mother, for example, she wanted several times to leave the Party. After a miscarriage during her first year of marriage she said to my father that she would like to go back to the city to become a doctor, but he urged her not to. He told her that she would have no future if she left, she would be discriminated against all her life. My mother didn't understand at the time, she didn't understand the full meaning of those days – that you never knew what was going to happen. But from the urgency in my father's tone she could sense it was a dangerous thing to do. There must have been a lot of people like my mother – with my father unfortunately I don't know now – but from the way he tried to persuade my mother I can see he probably had doubts too from a similar experience. So people's way out was cut off because tremendous pressure was put on them to co-operate and to think in certain directions.'

Jung herself embraced Communism when she was young, as everybody else did.

'When I was growing up there was a personality cult around Mao; he was like a god. In a way we were brainwashed because there was no information in those days. We were isolated from the rest of the world. The way people usually make up their minds – by reading newspapers, watching television, talking to their friends – we could do none of those things in China then. Parents could not tell their children anything different from the Party line because children might talk and in that case they would endanger the whole family. And also what's the point of bringing up your children to become nonconformists? They would only ruin their lives. So parents all over China who loved their children said to them, "Do as Chairman Mao says." And that reinforced the power of Mao's personality cult. Imagine a situation where you have no other input except Mao's words and only Mao as an object of worship. And it was all backed by coercion and terror anyway, so you couldn't do otherwise.

'So it wasn't a belief that even went through my conscious thinking. It worked on people's subconscious so you grew up taking it for granted, you grew up knowing no alternatives. Sometimes I think it must have been as simple as a biological conditioned reflex.'

Looking back later, Jung could see some of the reasons why the cult of Mao was so effective. For one thing it seemed to rectify the unhappy past which people still had many memories of: the Japanese invasion and the class-ridden days of Chiang Kai-shek when peasants starved. Those memories were why she and others were brought up to smash such enemies. Then too Mao cleverly conquered the high moral ground by presenting harshness to class enemies as loyalty to the people and total submission to him as a way of being selfless (many religious leaders demand such submission for the same ostensible reason). Thus he sowed the seeds for his own deification. He became a god and this accorded with the ancient Chinese tradition of the emperor figure, who was head of state and spiritual leader rolled into one.

Cleverly, Mao allowed himself to become remote, a mystery. Few people, except for his staff, ever actually met him and even his top officials only saw him in formal audience. Again, he fitted into a Chinese pattern, that of the saviour of the people who led a great uprising against a corrupt dynasty and became an illustrious and wise emperor with absolute authority. And in fact he did, as Jung points out, earn his god-emperor status for he brought peace and stability, at least to begin with. It was under him that the Chinese became a power in the world and could cease feeling humiliated at being Chinese. This mattered very much to them as their national pride was intensely important. And, in any case, because Mao was remote and there was a system of disinformation, the ordinary people could never know of his failures or even how much success was due to other leaders of the Party.

'He went further than most dictators in that he changed people's minds. There was no need for a KGB in China. You didn't have to force people to denounce each other if you could make them want to do it for themselves.'

It was against this background that Jung, when she was fourteen, decided to join the new Red Guards. A whole generation of teenagers like herself had now grown up expecting that they would have to fight class enemies. Some of them sensed that Mao himself, their god, might be in need of their help, and in 1966 these influential students had begun to call themselves the Red Guards of Chairman Mao. The first Red Guards were the children of high officials and were interested in politics and intrigue. Mao himself greatly approved of them and wrote an open letter offering his 'most warm and fiery support'. He told them that 'rebellion against reactionaries is justified'. To the students it was like being addressed by God and very soon Red Guard groups were springing up all over China.

Mao himself was never secure while the Communist Party was in authority. Although he was the leader and worshipped by the people, he knew that there could be intrigue against him by high Party officials. So he determined to remove authority from the Party and establish total obedience to himself alone. For this he knew he had to create terror – 'an intense terror that would block all other considerations and crush all other fears'. Boys and girls in their teens and early twenties were the ideal activists for they had been brought up with a fanatical loyalty to him, and they were rebellious and eager to fight for him, longing for adventure and action. 'They were the best agents,' says Jung, 'because teenagers are prone to violence; they are fearless and they have the instinct to fight for a just cause. Also they are rebellious and easy to manipulate. Only they could give Mao the immense force that he needed to terrorize the whole society, and to create a chaos that would shake, and then shatter, the foundation of the Party. Thus was the Cultural Revolution born. One slogan summed up the Red Guards' mission: "We vow to launch a bloody war against anyone who dares to resist the Cultural Revolution, who dares to oppose Chairman Mao."'

Now every form of violence was encouraged. Mao called on the Red Guards to smash up old ideas, old culture, old customs and old habits. Boys and girls took to the streets, giving full vent to their fanaticism. They tore apart people's houses, burning their antiques and their books. Soon, every private collection was destroyed and then they turned on the museums, the temples, the ancient tombs and statues – anything old was a target and in this way China lost practically all its treasures.

But Jung makes the point that not all the Red Guards were cruel or violent. It was a loose organization and it did not force its members to act savagely. Indeed, Mao himself never actually ordered the Red Guards to kill, and his instructions about violence were often contradictory. It was possible to be devoted to Mao without perpetrating violence. But there was an insidious encouragement of atrocities which fed the underlying desire for wild ferocity that was in many of the young.

'I was not forced to join the Red Guards,' says Jung. 'It just went without saying that I should join. No one forced you to join the Red Guards, we wanted to join. One reason was that the Red Guards were "Mao's babies" and another reason was that the teenagers wanted to belong to their peer group. You don't want to be rejected by your friends. Not joining the Red Guards was seen as a form of rejection of your peers.'

She tells us that nobody in those days was capable of rational thinking. Their minds were so cowed by fear that to deviate from Mao's directions was inconceivable. Everyone had been overwhelmed by wrong information, deceptive rhetoric and hypocrisy, so that it was impossible for ordinary people to see through such a situation and make any intelligent judgements.

People in Sichuan province, where Jung lived, had little idea of the terror and destruction in the big cities; and the Chengdu Red Guards in her home town, although they looted some houses, did not openly steal, so that life went on fairly normally. Jung was accepted by the Red Guards, wore the red armband embroidered with gold, and left home to live in the school with others. Her hair was cut short, she put patches on her trousers to look proletarian, but soon found herself dismayed by the destruction of the local temple and the burning of books. Nevertheless she shut her eyes to much of it, even when she was made to remove all the grass from the lawns because Mao had issued instructions that the growing of grass and flowers was a bourgeois habit to be eliminated. She still wrote passionate eulogies to Mao, thanking him for all he had done and pledging undying loyalty to him.

Indeed it became the purpose of her life to actually see Mao. Many of the young felt the same way and pilgrimages to gaze on the holy leader were encouraged – food, accommodation and transport were all free. But nothing was organized and when she and her friends – she was still only fourteen – arrived in Peking they were given very poor shelter and the crowds were such that when Mao passed through Tiananmen Square, Jung, who had fallen asleep after hours of waiting, saw only the back of him. 'I was so heartbroken that for a minute I thought should I commit suicide now that my life's purpose had been smashed?'

There was no more schooling for anyone after June 1966. 'When the Cultural Revolution started I was at school and in those days all proper teaching stopped. The books were either burnt or locked up because they didn't have Mao's quotations on every page. In any case, Mao had said "the more books you read, the more stupid you become". And of course he needed victims and Mao's first victims were the teachers. Through his propaganda machine Mao told the pupils that the teachers were conspiring with international capitalism to use things like exams to persecute the pupils, so this made some Red Guards violent towards the teachers – they felt their violence was justified and not only justified but virtuous. They felt righteous for beating up their teachers. No one protested because somehow the terror was such that you felt if you raised one voice of protest you would be crushed, you would be beaten to death. It was the atmosphere of the most terrible mob violence.

'My parents were senior Communist officials so they became enemies; they fell into the category of what was called the capitalist-roaders, those who took the capitalist way. It was the time when you could be beaten to death for saying just one word or being accused of saying one word against Mao or the Cultural Revolution. Throughout China millions of people were condemned for nothing. My parents, like most Communist officials, suddenly became class enemies.

'My father was one of the few who stood up to Mao and

153

condemned the Cultural Revolution. He wrote letters to Mao to protest. But when he was going to write to Mao my mother was very worried because, as she said to him, "Do you want our children to become blacks; do you want to ruin the future of our children?" And also she thought it was useless, writing those letters. But because of who he was, he would always support his principles before the interest of his family. He said, "What about the children of the victims?" He told my mother that he now realized the Cultural Revolution wasn't a revolution at all, but rather Mao wanted to get rid of the people who disagreed with him. So he wrote to Mao. He said the Cultural Revolution was creating chaos and many people were suffering terribly and this was against the principles of Marxism and against the principles of Communism.'

No arguments from his wife, who knew that this would mean imprisonment, could stop him. But before the letter could be sent, he was accused by local students of opposing the Cultural Revolution and after some months of constant public verbal attacks, the Red Guards came to the family's home and burnt all his books. By 1967 both Jung's parents were in and out of prison, her father for his condemnation of the Cultural Revolution and her mother because she refused to denounce her husband.

'My mother was under great pressure to denounce my father. But she was not going to desert him and she fought for him. At great personal risk she went twice to Peking to appeal on his behalf. She managed to see Xhou Enlai, who wrote her a note and secured my father's release from prison. Because of my father, my mother went through over a hundred denunciation meetings. She was detained, she was made to kneel on broken glass, she was tortured, she was sent to a labour camp, but she would not denounce her husband. So all this made me love my parents much more than before.'

Indeed, the whole family of five children became very close to each other. Because there was no schooling, they had a great deal of free time and Jung began to write poetry. This helped her to contemplate her existence in a more profound manner and was to be the key that began to open the door of her mind.

'The first poem with which I felt satisfied was written on my sixteenth birthday. There was no birthday celebration. Both my parents were in detention. That night, as I lay in bed listening to the gunshots and the loudspeakers blaring out bloodcurdling diatribes, I reached a turning point. I had always been told, and had believed, that I was living in a paradise on earth, socialist China, whereas the capitalist world was hell. Now I asked myself: If this is paradise, what then is hell? I decided that I would like to see for myself whether there was indeed a place more full of pain. For the first time, I consciously hated the regime I lived under, and craved an alternative.

'It was in this mood that I composed my poem. I wrote about the death of my indoctrinated and innocent past as dead leaves being swept from a tree by the whirlwind and cried to a world of no return. I described my bewilderment at the new world, at not knowing what and how to think. It was a poem of groping in the dark, searching.'

No sooner had she written the poem down than she heard a banging on the door and knew that it was a house raid. There had been previous raids and most of the 'bourgeois luxury items' such as her grandmother's elegant pre-Communist clothes had gone. She guessed now that they had come back to try to find evidence against her father and she was gripped with fear that if her poem were discovered, she too would be in terrible trouble. She rushed to the lavatory and flushed it away even while they pounded on the lavatory door.

In 1969 Jung and all her family were exiled, one after another, from their home in Chengdu and sent to work in labour camps in the countryside. Mao advocated 'thought-reform through labour' for everyone but never explained what that meant. Altogether some fifteen million young people were sent to the country and, with a suitcase and a bedroll, Jung went off with her school to the borders of the Himalayas. The conditions under which they lived were very primitive and they suffered unbearably from the cold. The work was done by hand – there were not even any farm animals because the peasants were too poor to be able to afford them. Water and fuel were difficult to get and demanded long and exhausting trudges. But hardship was supposed to be part of the 'thought-reform' and in theory had to be relished as bringing one closer to the birth of a new person.

'Before the Cultural Revolution, I had subscribed wholeheartedly to this attitude, and had deliberately done hard work in order to make myself a better person ... Now, scarcely three years later, instead of making me more loyal to Mao, my experience opened my eyes to reality. Peasants' lives were extremely hard; they had to work every minute of their waking hours.' Her indoctrination was collapsing. Without the psychological support of blind belief, she found herself appalled by the hardships she and the others had to endure, and began to feel it was utterly pointless.

Jung became ill and was allowed to leave the village to go home. Her grandmother was still in their house and gave her Chinese medicines and nourishing meals. She was soon much better. But in order to stay at home she needed documents and the only way to get these was to go back to the village. This she accomplished, but when she returned to Chengdu her beloved grandmother had died. She had been very ill but had not received proper medical treatment because hospitals had collapsed in the Cultural Revolution. It was a great blow to Jung.

'I've often dreamed of my grandmother since. She was a wonderful person, vivacious, talented and immensely capable. It was always she who had held the family together and looked after everybody.'

Jung was not allowed to live on her own and it was now necessary for her to join a commune. She was accepted for peasant work once more but this time the place was less primitive and although there were no machines, the work was a little lighter. But she was shaken to discover that even before the Cultural Revolution the Communist Party had forced the peasants to smash their woks and stoves so that the metal could be fed into the furnaces. Most of their grain was taken from them for the cities and they, the villagers, had died in scores.

'The peasants' stories shook me to the core. It was the first time I had come across the ugly side of Communist China before the Cultural Revolution. The picture was vastly different from the rosy official version. In the hills and fields of Deyang my doubts about the Communist regime deepened.

'I have sometimes wondered whether Mao knew what he was doing putting the sheltered urban youth of China in touch with reality. But then he was confident that much of the population would not be able to make rational deductions with the fragmentary information available to them. Indeed, at the age of eighteen, I was still only capable of vague doubts, not explicit analysis of the regime. No matter how much I hated the Cultural Revolution, to doubt Mao still did not enter my mind.'

Jung spent much of her time visiting the different parts of the country where her parents were and this made her unpopular with the commune. She seized the chance to become a 'barefoot doctor' when the training was available and joined a clinic, built on its own at the top of a hill. Here, for almost the first time, she found a degree of solitude, one that she welcomed very much.

'I enjoyed living on that hilltop, far away from any village. Every morning, I got up early, strolled along the edge of the hill, and to the rising sun recited lines from an ancient book of verse about acupuncture. Beneath my feet, the fields and cottages began to wake up to the cock's crowing. A lonely Venus watched with a pale glow from a sky that was getting brighter every minute. I loved the fragrance of the honeysuckle in the morning breeze, and the big petals of nightshade shaking off pearls of dew. Birds chirped all around, distracting me from my recitations. I would linger for a bit, and then walk back to light my stove for breakfast.'

Throughout her troubled young life, Jung had always longed for solitude. The constant bombarding of slogans through loudspeakers in the streets, the perpetual need to show oneself an active person in the community and not one given to introspection, the growing up in a compound made up of a number of families living close together – these conditions had not quenched her longing for aloneness but had fuelled it, even though when she was alone she felt inclined to think 'heretical' thoughts. Now she understands this impulse.

'I have realized that the human mind – not just me – the human mind is such a wonderful thing that it would insist on thinking for itself, it would try to draw conclusions from its own experience. It would have a capacity of finding, or reaching out for bits of information. That applied to reading the books that escaped the bonfires of the Red Guard. One of my brothers discovered a black market set of books and I was able to read them.

'If you have a strong wish to be left alone, as I did, I believe it's because you have inner resources to think for yourself – therefore you are more inclined to have doubts and to question. And your mind is constantly discovering information and trying to come to its own conclusions. For instance, there was a time when I first thought the West must be a wonderful place. No one from the West had put this idea into my mind – indeed, there was all the regime's denunciation of the West. But you suddenly realize that you like all the things they denounce the West for – so your mind independently reaches this conclusion. And another time when we went on a pilgrimage to Mao's birthplace and I suddenly realized that Mao's parents must be the so-called "rich peasants" who were supposed to be the enemies of the revolution. So my mind said, why were Mao's parents revered, whereas all other rich peasants were denounced and killed as enemies?

'So I began to think independently when I was alone, and I hated the constant pressure of people all the time – that was the most difficult thing in China. And the intrusion into your life, criticizing it. And of course in those days it was not simple intrusion, not just being nosy, but the nosiness had political dimensions.'

Underlying Jung's commitment to Communism, and fed by her occasional moments of being alone, was a sense of herself as a poet and also perhaps as a mystic. She loved the countryside and found in it a timeless, healing quality, utterly different from everyday life. On one of the rare occasions when she was alone in the fields, for instance, she began composing a poem and found that the universe seemed to be standing still. That sense of timelessness gave her the feeling that life was intrinsically beautiful.

'I think one's love of beauty must perhaps be instinctive – there's more in some people and less in others. For me, I always felt an affinity with nature and took intense pleasure in its beauty. And in those days I lived in political persecutions all around me and those persecutions were carried out by people. So getting away from people and into nature was a way of retreating from that sub-human conduct.

'Also in the Chinese culture – and I am thinking of poets – there is a tremendous worshipping of nature. In the tradition I was brought up in nature was sacred and it was a subject of inspiration and reverence. The moon, the sun, the dew, the wind, they are all meaningful. They are not just pleasing to your eye, they also please your emotions. They have connections with your spirit and even your sense of logic, your ideas. It came to be a constant source for my inner resourcefulness and food for my thinking and my feeling.'

Indeed, Chinese painters and poets of old had always believed that the landscape was able to express the Way, the spiritual truth, to those who could receive it. To wander in the landscape, among mountains and streams was a means of drawing closer to the mysteries of the cosmos.

'There is an eternity in nature and that somehow is healing in the sense that you feel there must be other things that are eternal. Then the ugliness, the violence and the awfulness of human behaviour can become like fleeting clouds, they come and they go. That understanding was very healing, it was a reprieve for me.

'When I was fifteen, I was able to climb to the tops of two sacred mountains in Sichuan. I went to the Yellow Mountain which is a Buddhist sacred mountain. The Yellow Mountain was a place for Buddhist pilgrims but when I was there, there were very few of them because if they were caught they were treated harshly. There were monks there and I could talk to them, but they were made to run their temples like hotels. They had to entertain, to provide food and so on for people such as myself. But there was another mountain in Sichuan, a Taoist sacred mountain and I loved it very much. I knew the names of Taoism and Buddhism but I didn't know exactly what they meant and what were their principles. So one day I worked out their ideas. But if you go to the sacred mountains, as I did, you become in touch with the religion. There were monks on the Yellow Mountain and there were Taoist priests on the other mountain and I had long talks with them. It was very tranquil, like another way of life. It was a retreat in those days and I found it extremely peaceful.'

So Jung fed herself, almost unwittingly, with the experiences that would one day help her to emerge with her spirit intact into a wider world. It seems surprising that she was allowed to go to such places but she tells us that there were no barriers. 'In the Cultural Revolution control actually collapsed to a large extent, so people did have a measure of personal freedom and could go to many places. You needed some kind of identification, perhaps a letter of introduction, but it was not impossible to get these documents. I don't think it was intentional that people should have this freedom, but it happened.

The breakdown of society gave people both more personal freedom and more personal responsibility. Some people used the freedom to see China and some used it to read. But many used it to be engaged in violence, in fighting, and in political persecutions.'

In 1972, after the death of Lin Bao, a marshal who had attempted to assassinate Mao, Mao initiated a rehabilitation of many Party officials. This was not through sudden feelings of leniency but because with Lin gone, and with almost every other marshal alienated from him, he had to turn to the purged leaders who still commanded the loyalty of the army. The first concession he had to make was to bring back most of the denounced officials. Suddenly Jung's father had all his salary returned to him as well as his possessions. The family were able to come back to Chengdu. Jung's mother found her daughter a place in a factory making machine tools and for some months Jung became an apprentice electrician. But the biggest change was that she was allowed to start reading books again. She visited Peking for some months and was able to read about Western ideas and politics and when she went back to the factory she decided to prepare herself for a university course. She studied the major subjects, for at that time students were assigned to courses with no consideration for what they were interested in. At last, in October 1973, she entered the Foreign Languages Department of Sichuan University to study English.

In the meantime Mme Mao and her cohorts – the Gang of Four – whom Mao had put in charge of virtually every area, tried to prevent the country from working. Slogans appeared such as 'To stop production is revolution itself'; and, for agriculture, 'We would rather have socialist weeds than capitalist crops'. Acquiring foreign technology became 'Sniffing after foreigner's farts and calling them sweet'; and, in education, 'We want illiterate working people not educated spiritual aristocrats'. An attempt was made to start the Cultural Revolution again, with schoolchildren encouraged to rebel against their teachers; and the whole country began to close up again after a period when it looked as though it would be more open to the rest of the world.

'It was in this period,' says Jung, 'that I started to realize that it was Mao who was really responsible for the Cultural Revolution. But

I still did not condemn him explicitly, even in my own mind. It was so difficult to destroy a god!'

In the meantime she was having great difficulty learning English at university for there were no native English speakers about since the whole of Sichuan was closed to foreigners and people could be put in prison for listening to the BBC. The textbooks were all propaganda and the first English sentence they learned was 'Long live Chairman Mao!' With great difficulty Jung managed to borrow some pre-Cultural Revolution English textbooks from lecturers but she had to keep them hidden. The next difficulty was that she was better at English than her classmates, who mostly came from a peasant background, and she was soon accused of being 'bourgeois'. She was also accused of being aloof and cutting herself off from the masses when she wanted to study by herself. 'It was common in China for people to say that you must be looking down on them if you failed to hide your desire for some solitude.'

But when at last she could read English she found a treasury of books in the university library, for most of the books burnt in the past had been Chinese. She read novels and philosophy and says, 'My joy at the sensation of my mind opening up and expanding was beyond description.

'Being alone in the library was heaven for me. My heart would leap as I approached it, usually at dusk, anticipating the pleasure of solitude with my books, the outside world ceasing to exist. As I hurried up the flight of stairs, into the pastiche classical-style building, the smell of old books long stored in airless rooms would give me tremors of excitement, and I would hate the stairs for being so long.'

One day a friend showed her a copy of *Newsweek* with an article on the Maos in it. The friend wanted to know what the article said. One sentence struck Jung like a flash of lightning – Mme Mao was Mao's 'ears, eyes and voice'. Up till then she had refused to allow herself to accept the obvious connection between the way Mme Mao inflicted suffering and Mao himself. Now it suddenly became clear to her that it was Mao who had been behind all the destruction and misery because without him the Gang of Four could not have lasted a day. For the first time she challenged Mao openly in her mind. 'When I first came to contemplate doubting him, to spelling out his name in my mind, I was quite shocked. It was a mixture of tremendous thrill and tremendous horror – you feel you've gone cold because of your terror.'

She was not alone. As Mao's health began to fail and his grip to weaken, irreverent graffiti began to appear scribbled on walls and on the slogans that covered the walls. 'There was once a great tradition of humour in China and especially in the part that I came from – in Sichuan.' Her own brother Jin-ming made her laugh with his sceptical comments and it was his irreverence that helped destroy her rigid ways of thinking. 'To be able to think in a sceptical way was my first step to enlightenment.

'But for a long time humour was dangerous and people were terrified and dared not express this side of themselves. The first time I saw this sort of humour coming back publicly was at what they called the first Tiananmen incident in April 1976 when people gathered in Tiananmen Square and openly defied the regime. In those days there were giant slogans on the walls, each written character would be the size of a man. Now people started scribbling graffiti on the margins of the slogans and some of it was very irreverent and funny. They were very brave. And also at this point Mao's control wasn't as tight as before, because he was near his last days, so the regime was on the point of collapse. And after ten years people were *so* fed up. Everybody was, including some of the hardliners such as the police and the army. So people were able to write these irreverent graffiti. One was "Deep fry Deng Xiaoping". "Deep fry" was funny because the monthly oil ration was only ten per cent of a kilo, so what would you use to deep fry Deng Xiaoping? It was funny but it was very daring and frightening too.'

In 1976 Mao died. When she heard the news Jung was filled with great euphoria, although her sense of self-preservation immediately registered that everyone was weeping and she had better try to do so herself. She started to do a lot of thinking about his whole regime. He had brought out and nourished the worst in people. 'Mao had created a moral wasteland and a land of hatred. But how much individual responsibility ordinary people should share, I could not decide.'

After the Gang of Four were eliminated, China began to change for the better. Jung was given the post of assistant lecturer in the university and when the opportunity to compete for a foreign scholarship came up, she won it – the first woman in Sichuan ever to do so – and was accepted to go to York University in Great Britain.

This enormous and momentous change came after the death of her father and as she sat in Chengdu Airport she kept thinking how proud of her both he and her grandmother would have been. And later she thought of her mother. 'When I was finally slumped in my seat I realized I had hardly given my mother a proper hug. She had come to see me off at Chengdu Airport, almost casually, with no trace of tears, as though my going half a globe away was just one more episode in our eventful lives.'

Jung has frequently returned to China to visit her mother but her home is now in Britain. She is married to Jon Halliday, a specialist in Far Eastern affairs, and together they are working on a biography of Mao. Jung herself is a woman of presence and beauty and her home is simple and elegant, with fine Chinese furniture and a balcony looking out on to green gardens. It was to this tall London house that her mother came for a visit which was to last six months, and to result in the writing of *The Wild Swans*, for her mother told Jung a great deal she did not know about the past. 'I didn't really understand my mother before I wrote the book. The process of writing it was also a process of getting to know my father and also my grandmother and I felt much closer to them.

'My mother could feel this and in one of her letters to me before the publication of the book she said that the book might not do very well and people might not pay attention to it, but I was not to be disheartened because she could see that writing the book had made me love her more and this for her was enough.'

Although her mother has returned to stay in China, two of Jung's brothers and their families now live in England, and another brother is in France. Only her elder sister has remained with her mother in China.

The Wild Swans is, and will remain, an epic account of a young girl's search for truth and integrity, for a sense of meaning and of the sacred in a fiercely repressive regime. Her god failed her in the end and she saw through him – but he was a god and she did worship him with the strength of a fervent young heart.

Now she can look at things peacefully and in perspective and she can let go all the tense defences that dominated her life. 'When I first came to Britain I felt I could relax. Even though it was like another planet and everything was different and, although I could read Dickens, I could barely speak – I couldn't even ask for a cup of tea – yet I felt at home. And one thing I felt was wonderful, I was left alone.

'Britain is a very peaceful place because there has been no war for so long, and I love the tranquillity. Also, the scenery in Britain is not dramatic but there's a gentleness – trees, grass and colour – it calms you down and gives you a feeling of harmony.'

Harmony was a condition she had longed for in her earlier life, but when she left China and looked back over the years of her youth, she saw that she had experienced privileges even if the denunciation had been all the more severe, courage in spite of the terror, and she had seen kindness and loyalty, as well as the depths of human ugliness.

'Amid suffering, ruin and death, I had above all known love and the indestructible human capacity to survive, and to pursue happiness.'

Sheila Cassidy

'There's a sense in which I think all the world is holy because all the world is permeated by God. The sacred is the transcendent, the God in things, the God in people, the immanence of God. I'm always lured by the sacred and I'm always lured by spiritual people, whatever their religion, and by people who pray seriously. I'm lured too by sacred places – abbeys, monasteries, cathedrals. And I'm driven wild by plainchant, I'm driven wild by God.'

Sheila Cassidy is deeply committed to a life based on her belief in God. She is a Roman Catholic but her sense of God is not always one the Church would share; it is as unconventional and as urgently alive as she is herself and she has little time for the over-simple adorations of the pious.

'I find myself very ill at ease with traditional Catholic spirituality – devotion to the Sacred Heart, devotion to the Mother of God. Our Lady in a pale blue scarf really turns me off. I find my spiritual resource in such things as the language of emptiness of God, books like *The Cloud of Unknowing* and physical things like an empty cathedral. I would love to lie flat on the floor and pray in a completely empty cathedral with no people, no chairs, no anything. There's something very special about nothingness; it seems to be enormously important spiritually.

'In the same way, I often pray in the dark and I pray without words most of the time. The paradoxical and negative language of God is what I love. I can't be doing with the language of gentle Jesus. I have a sense of the violence of God, the fire of God, the wildness of God.

'There is a distinction between people who are God-centred and those who are Christ-centred and I am very deeply God-centred. There are times when I think I'm barely Christian. But in fact this isn't so, because when I actually get forced to read the Gospel it is very precious to me and I suppose my roots in Christianity are deep.

'But I have difficulty with the suffering of Jesus in the Gospels because of my own experience of physical suffering and I find the two things get in the way of each other in a sense. I think, though, that the Christian idea of God being in the tortured prisoner or the person dying of Aids is very meaningful to me. When I was afraid and suffering, I tried desperately to pray and I asked, What do I have to give you? And all I had to give was my pain.'

Sheila's pain was a turning point in her life. She is a medical doctor and during her late twenties she was put in charge of a casualty department in a big hospital. But she was frustrated by the administration which meant she had no opportunity for the training in surgery that she had always wanted. She became friends with a young doctor from Chile, Consuelo, who was working in the department. When Consuelo returned to Chile, Sheila decided to follow her and to continue her surgical training in South America. She emphasizes that at this point in her life she was entirely materialistic. She had heard that a doctor in Chile would have maids and a swimming pool, and did not conceive that she would have any desire to serve the poor. Her decision to go there, however, was to have consequences she could never have dreamed of.

When she arrived in Chile with her dog and all her household goods, she found a country in political turmoil – although for at least six months she was quite unaware of it as she could not speak any Spanish. In the end Consuelo explained to her that the Allende government was trying to bring about in five years the sort of welfare state that it took England a hundred years to establish. They were trying to tackle hunger and malnutrition, illiteracy and sub-human housing, but there was great opposition to many of Allende's reforms from those who were happy with the status quo.

But still Sheila did not take much notice of the politics. As well as learning Spanish she also had to retake some of her exams in order to practise medicine in Chile and she, Consuelo and another doctor who shared a house, were poor and needed all the work they could get. By 1973, though, after she had lived in Santiago for two years, had completed her exams and had conquered Spanish, Sheila was established in surgery. But she was then appalled by a general strike of doctors – which was in fact a trigger leading to the final division of Chile. At first Sheila went as usual to the hospital but the Medical College decided that the work done by foreign doctors was impeding the effectiveness of the strike and she was ordered to stay at home. A month later there was a military coup and Allende's government was ousted. Sheila was at home listening to the radio with Consuelo when she heard the voice of the new rulers of Chile issuing orders to the people. 'Every station carried the same voice. Free speech had ended.'

There followed a reign of terror. The new government bombed the centre of Santiago to destroy the government buildings. 'In less than a day the vision of the new Chile was destroyed along with the man who had believed that he could bring about a redistribution of wealth in his country without the spilling of blood. Allende's had not been the violent way of Fidel Castro or Che Guevara: he had believed that he could achieve a bloodless revolution but he had not reckoned with the CIA's investment of eight million dollars to bring down his government nor with the triumph of the latent fascism in a certain sector of the Chilean middle class.'

Life took on a new pattern and fear ruled the country.

'In the early days of the military dictatorship there was violence and terror everywhere. Thousands were killed and thousands more were herded like cattle into the massive football stadium. No one was allowed out after eight at night and as I looked along the darkened streets of a Santiago under curfew I would see the sleek limousines of the military, the long fast cars, racing towards the centre of the city, followed by lorries full of soldiers, or tanks. Helicopters surveyed the city each night and bus-loads of steel-helmeted soldiers would speed away to assignments searching for the "terrorists". And always lurking in the shadows would be the stealthy figures with machine guns.'

After some weeks Sheila was allowed to return to work but was deeply saddened by the death of Consuelo from a fatal illness. Sheila's religion had not meant much to her for some years but now she felt sad and lonely. She 'quietly and naturally' returned to her undergraduate practice of daily attendance at mass and communion. And the church that she rediscovered in Santiago in 1974 was very different in character from the one she had left in Leicester in the mid 1960s. It wasn't just the liturgy that was more alive, but the people.

'The first two priests I met were American missionaries who lived in a shanty town on the outskirts of Santiago. They lived in a small wooden house among the very poor people and I felt I wanted to become part of what they were doing and fighting for. I was to meet many more of these lean men and women in the months to come – shabby tigers in their dusty boots. It was with them that I learned to pray again, to read the scriptures and to recognize in the psalms the anger, pain and joy of an oppressed people.'

As a medical student she had felt a strong call to become a nun but then she had fallen in love and the call had been pushed aside. Now, once more, she again and incredulously felt the same call to be a nun. She was afraid and distressed by such an idea for she had grown to love the work she was doing. She asked advice from a priest who told her to live with the calling for a while, to see if it was the right one. By this time, also, she had made good friends in the missionary community among the nuns and priests, the 'liberation theologists' who believed that the military Junta was an offence against Christianity, and she did nothing about her calling for the time being.

The Church had started a plan for small clinics in shanty towns and now she was asked to leave the hospital and work in one. But she had always enjoyed the life of a big hospital and felt reluctant to give it up. She says, 'I knew then that this was a crucial moment. If I opted to keep my satisfying work in good conditions when there were people in desperate need of a doctor, I could not say in truth that I was committed to the service of the under-privileged. It was true enough that I would be wasting my specialist training, but it was also true that there were enough doctors in this field [of plastic surgery] and a great shortage of those prepared to practise simple general medicine amongst the poor. So it was that with the same bad grace that I had accepted the calling to be a nun, I now accepted the bishop's invitation to work in the clinic.

'It amazes me now that it took so long for the political reality to dawn on me – the direct link between people's health and their social conditions. I think the penny had really dropped for me when I was working in a children's hospital. Each day we would admit a number of sick babies, tiny, wizened creatures, half the size they should be because they were not getting enough to eat. I remember to this day how the doctors stood round the cots and discussed the management of such cases as if it was pneumonia or meningitis or cancer, but not malnourishment and illness caused by poverty. At this stage I had been angry with the system but I too was poor and had no sense of responsibility.

'Now, in Chacabuco, I began to work with the marginal people of Chile and as the weeks passed I grew to love them. Drunk they may have been, alcoholics, rogues and prostitutes they certainly were, but they were a warm people who asked little and accepted gratefully what we could do for them . . . A few of them brought me gifts, the more moving because they were so poor. Occasionally I became personally involved with them and was made desperate by the enormity of their problems and my inability to solve them.

'As I spent more time in prayer and tried to translate my growing love of God into concrete terms, I sought Him more and more in my patients, mindful of Matthew 25: "I was sick and you visited me". I tried hard to be more caring and more gentle and much of the time it worked, though when I was tired or hungry or harassed my good intentions and humour left me and I was impatient and unfriendly.

'It was easy to see the image of God in the sun setting behind the Andes or behind the restless tossing of the sea, but the image of Christ in his creatures is a very tarnished one and it is too easy to miss.

'As the weeks turned into months and I persevered with my search and extended my hours of prayer to include the bus journey to work and odd moments when I wasn't busy, I found that my patience was rewarded and I came to see Him more and more in the broken ones of Santiago.'

And then the moment came for the greatest test in her faith. Early one morning a Chilean priest friend asked her if she would be prepared to treat a man with a bullet wound in his leg.

'So now it had happened. The moment that I had neither looked forward to nor dreaded had arrived, as I had known that it inevitably would. Without hesitating I said yes, knowing quite well that this might mean the end of my work in Chile. I did not weigh up the pros and cons: a doctor faced with a wounded man does not weigh on balance the worth of that man against the worth of other possible patients . . . Anyway, I had no doubts; it was not my place to judge this man but to treat him.'

Nelson Gutierrez, a revolutionary, was being given refuge in a convent. But Sheila could not extract the bullet from his leg without the equipment of an operating theatre and she recommended that he be taken to the Papal Nuncio where he would be safe as it had embassy status, and then transferred to a hospital. Two days later she was asked to visit him again, this time in the Nunciatura, but on arrival was told to her relief that he was being looked after by other doctors.

A week after she had treated Gutierrez, she heard that he was safely in asylum. That evening she was in the house of some missionary friends, praying with a sick nun. Suddenly there was a terrible scream.

'I rushed to the landing, thinking that perhaps Enriquetta the housekeeper must have fallen down the stairs. Indeed there she was, lying on the dining room floor, but with blood flowing from a bullet wound in her back. My memories of the next few minutes are like a bad gangster movie, trying to staunch the flow of blood and then taking cover, cringing under the kitchen table from a fresh hail of bullets. Then, to my amazement, I found it was me they had come for and they led me blindfold to a waiting car.'

The soldiers took her to the Casa Grimaldi, a major interrogation centre of the dreaded DINA, the Directorate of National Intelligence. She was led into a room and ordered to take off all her clothes. Outraged, she protested that she was a British doctor and that this would cause an international incident. But the chilling reply was that DINA's image in the world was so bad that they didn't care. She took off her clothes. Her blindfold was a little loose and she could see that there were five men in the room, which contained only a table, a chair and a metal bunk.

They told her to lie on the bed and secured her, tying her wrists and ankles to the frame so that she was spread out with her legs apart. A wide band was put round her chest and abdomen and a gag thrust into her mouth. She felt an electric shock pass through her and then another and another.

Then the interrogation began. They wanted to know where she had treated Gutierrez and who had asked her to do so. With her head quite clear she made the decision to lie in order to save the nuns and priests involved. Also she did not believe that the treatment would go on for long, for she knew that the friends she left behind would have informed the British consul. Her lies were so convincing that they untied her and took her with them to the house she had described as part of her story. They could not of course find it and told her that it would be much easier for them if they killed her straight away.

'I sat there and realized that perhaps I was going to die. It was a curious feeling and I thought, what then? Suddenly God and heaven seemed very unreal and very far away and I wondered seriously, almost for the first time in my life, if it was all a fairy story. It was as though I looked over the edge of a precipice and saw nothing and it seemed that there was nothing beyond. I can't remember what I thought over the next few minutes but I know that I came back quite calmly to the certainty that it was not all nonsense and that God did exist, but this was a coldblooded intellectual decision and it brought me no warm Christian comfort.

'As I faced the prospect of death I thought, what a very stupid way to die. But there seemed no alternative to what I was doing, so I sat there and somehow stretched out my hand to the God who seemed so far away.'

As she was proved to have lied, they took her back to the room with the bunk and once more she was splayed out on the bed, the ropes and straps tied so tightly that her circulation was severely impeded. 'During the first interrogation I never knew where the electrodes had been placed and the pain was generalized. Now they became more sophisticated for one electrode was placed inside my vagina and the other, a wandering pincer, was used to stimulate me wherever they chose.'

This time the pain was appalling and they interrogated with a speed and ferocity that allowed no possibility of making anything up. So gradually she answered their questions, trying not to say too much. But they found the truth more difficult to believe than her previous story because they could not believe that nuns and priests were involved.

'Their disbelief was very hard to bear for there seemed no escape from the white hot sea of pain in which I found myself. Terrifying too was the increased callousness of the interrogators. Each time they passed the current a gag was forced into my mouth and I was told, "Raise your finger when you are ready to talk." Unable to cry out and with my hands nearly paralysed I could call for relief only through the upward movement of my finger and this they ignored, filling me with a desperation the like of which I have never known.

'How long it went on I don't know: perhaps an hour, perhaps longer. I told them that I had treated Nelson Gutierrez in the house of some American nuns but I didn't know the address, for although I knew the street name I didn't know the number. Still furious, they realized that in truth I could not tell them where to go and once more they untied me . . .'

This time they found the house, but the two nuns who lived there were away. They had expected to find Gutierrez there too but when Sheila told them he had been given asylum in the Nunciatura they were enraged. So many people had become involved that they didn't know who to arrest. By now they were convinced that Sheila was working for the revolutionary movement, the MIR, and although she told them repeatedly that she had only treated Gutierrez because it was her duty to do so as a doctor, they could not believe this simple ethic. As the trail which had seemed so promising was now cold, they took her back to the torture room.

For the third time she was stripped and tied to the bed. They were convinced she knew where the MIR leader was and of course she had no idea. The pain now seemed more and more terrible and as they questioned her about every event of the day, they dragged out of her the names of the nuns and a certain priest who had been taking two other fugitives into asylum the previous night.

When they found that yet another church group was involved, they were even more furious. One group went off to search and while they were gone Sheila was taken to be interrogated by senior officers. But unable to get any more information from her they returned her to the torture room. Twice more she was stripped and tied to the bed but although she spent a long time lying cold and terrified on the bunk, they did not give her any more shocks.

'I think it was during this time of waiting that I was conscious of praying. I remember little except that I prayed for strength to withstand the pain and for courage to die with dignity if that was to be my fate. Most of all I remember a curious feeling of sharing in Christ's passion. Sick and numb with pain and fear, and spread-eagled so vulnerably on the bunk, it came to me that this was perhaps a little how it had been for him . . . And I had the feeling that God was there with me, not in any sense as a rescuer or a helper, but as a powerless bystander. I didn't feel for a moment that God had deserted me, but I had a sense that either he was powerless to help me or it wasn't in his purpose. If God is for real then that has to be so, because he doesn't come in shining armour and rescue everybody who's being tortured or dying of cancer.'

But at last she was taken out of the room and had to go through many more hours of interrogation. She was always afraid they would return her to the torture room but they did not. Instead she had to write a long dictated statement which began 'I . . . swear this statement is made without any form of duress.' Finally they took her to a cell and thus she began two months of imprisonment.

'When I was in prison I had two options. One was to scream like a child – "let me out, let me out" – which was a perfectly legitimate option. And the other was to try and say, whatever you want, so be it. Thy will be done. And I think that kind of option is there for a lot of people in a trap situation – I think one has the option to try to accept.'

She was not alone in prison though and those months remain for her a strange mixture of love and fear, for although the threat of the torture room and also of execution was never absent, she came to know and value the women with her – journalists, nuns, doctors and nurses – in a way that was unique. Tortured and imprisoned for their involvement with the poor or the banned political left, they formed a community and shared everything of their possessions. There were not enough beds or clothes but they gave to each other without thought. When Sheila at last returned to Chile many years later, it was these women she went to see.

Sheila's case was to come to court and the British consul, who became a good friend, advised her not to speak of her treatment or she would be punished for anything she said. While in prison her sense of the presence of God had remained with her and when at last she was expelled from Chile, and put on the plane for England, she knew that the religious life was waiting for her.

But first she had to make known the plight of those she had left behind. Although she was not able to speak out in Chile and always put on a smiling face for the press in case she was detained longer, now that she was home she pledged herself to fight for the release of all those prisoners, humiliated and afraid, that she had left behind. 'This was my chance to speak out and I would take it. I would be a voice for the voiceless, their ambassador to England.'

That mission took her to the House of Commons, the US Senate and the United Nations. She says, 'I lectured to bishops and seminarians, to doctors and medical students, and I've preached in more churches and cathedrals than I can remember. I've been hailed both as a martyr and a Marxist.' After sixteen months of such publicity she retired to heal herself and to study theology in the contemplative atmosphere of Ampleforth, a Benedictine monastery. From there, in due course, she went at last to a convent to become a nun. But it did not work!

Life in the convent was quite different from the intellectual stimulation and meditative atmosphere of Ampleforth, where she had been allowed to attend a number of theological classes for priests. She felt lonely for kindred spirits at the convent, and longed for the women of the prison camp with their vitality, warmth and courage. She felt constrained by the demands of a polite, all female society.

'It seemed that everything I did was wrong and I found myself unable to conform without intolerable strain. After eighteen months I was asked to leave because I was so unhappy and I know now they were right. At the time, however, I thought I could make it work because I did not realize that I am personally unsuited to community life. I had the calling to prayer, but not in a convent. I got very caged up, like a lion – I could have eaten them all!

'So the convent threw me out and I returned to the world to lick my wounds. Not to be outwitted in my attempts to be holier than everyone, I set myself up as a hermit on my brother's farm ... This worked well for about six weeks and then I ran out of money. At first I determined to do a few surgeries to earn my keep but I soon realized I was unfitted even for this and that the only thing I could do was to be a junior resident in a hospital. It wasn't difficult to get a locum post, and in July 1980 I returned to British medicine after a gap of nine years.

'To my great surprise and inner laughter, I found myself completely at home. No one seemed to mind the way I walked or dressed and no one complained about my language. To my amazement I found they valued the way I worked with patients and within a week I had been offered a permanent post. Slowly, I realized that I had come home. The hospital corridor was my cloister and my heart sang with thanksgiving as I clattered noisily down it. Here at last in my white coat and bright shirts I merged into the crowd and no one minded that my desk was cluttered or that I was always breathlessly a few minutes late instead of serenely early.'

After eighteen months of working on the cancer wards in a general hospital Sheila was offered a job as Medical Director of a new hospice for the dying, and in 1982 she took up the post. She soon found that she was, quite inadvertently, acquiring her own community and she acquired an even wider one when she began to write her books, to preach worldwide and to become a known figure on radio and television. Since her time in Chile, Sheila had felt herself deeply involved with those in pain and with those who are confined and powerless. But in the hospice she was to learn the limitations of what she could do to help.

'I work with people who are in hell dying from cancer or AIDS or Alzheimer's. That is my calling. I bring them what comfort I can, water to soothe their parched lips, a salve for blistered wounds, opium to relieve pain, but I can't free them. My pass through the locked gates is in my name only. I can come and go at will, but no one may leave with me. That, I suppose, is *my* greatest pain. I long to make a break for it, carrying these frail and wounded victims on my back until we are safely across the river, out of reach of the guards. But that, alas, can't be. Mine is simply the role of prison visitor, of comforter, of companion: I don't hold the keys. The liberator will come in his own good time, not in theirs, nor yet in mine . . .

'Working with the dying is a messy business, both physically and emotionally. People vomit or need the commode just when one is discussing some vital spiritual issue. They get fed up or tired after a very few minutes and make it clear that they've had enough. It takes quite a while, then, to tune into this sort of work, to give counsel when it's asked for – and be silent when it's not. It takes time, too, to learn to be content with just a few sentences, to relax and be a hollow instrument in God's hands so that the words and the music are his, not ours.

'People often ask me if my life in Chile has prepared me in any way for the work I do. I'm quite sure it has. The most important thing about the whole prison experience was that for me it was a time of special growth. I dare to say that I'm supremely grateful for what happened to me, though I'm beginning to understand that I shall never be rid of its scars. I'm grateful because it taught me so much about life and myself and about the extraordinary goodness of people. It taught me that life is a gift – that my health, my sanity, my freedom, all the things which I used to take for granted, are not mine by right. More than anything it taught me that we are created, sojourners in a land we did not make. You don't have to spend two months in a Chilean jail to learn this, any experience of powerlessness will do. An accident, an unexpected disaster, can destroy the illusion that we are in control of our lives.

'I found the experience of psychological powerlessness was painful, more terrifying than anything. And yet perversely I'm grateful for it, because it equips me to accompany those I care for. If one has experienced pain or depression or bereavement one is somehow a better companion. One can take the frightened hand or simply sit in silence. It's what's known in Third World jargon as solidarity, a very special sort of ministry to the powerless. But the best preparation is to have experienced powerlessness oneself.'

Sheila's belief in God came to sustain her totally but she could see that others were not so sustained. 'This is the light,' she says, 'by which I walk, the strength which makes it possible to live my life "on the margins of the bearable". But how can it work in practice? What do I say? How do I get over to people that God loves them?

'The answer, of course, is complex. There is no simple formula for pastoral care, nor can one single person do it all. Dying people are both needy and vulnerable, human beings stripped of their protection, naked and embarrassed like a snail without its shell or a moulting bird. They are physically weak, unpleasing to the eye, men and women of sorrows, acquainted with grief. The fact that there is a deep mystical meaning in suffering, which I do believe, does not for one moment say that suffering isn't really awful. To be losing half your genitalia, to be incontinent, to be mute, these things are terrible and people are very scared and unhappy. Frequently, they are disfigured, hard to look upon, people to make us screen our faces, all too easily despised and rejected by their fellows.

'What such people need, therefore, and what we must try to provide, is a place of refuge, a space both physical and emotional where they can feel safe, accepted just as they are. To be accepted, however, is only the beginning, for beyond acceptance we all need to be valued, to know that we have worth, to be loved . . . If I were to sum up our pastoral care in the hospice, I would say that we *reveal to people that they are lovable.*'

Sheila has found a great deal of help for her own wounds in psychotherapy and she agrees wholeheartedly with the psychologist Carl Rogers who talks of 'unconditional positive regard' by which he means 'I will accept whatever you bring to me. There is nothing that you can say which will make me reject you.' Sheila believes that this is *the* divine attribute. It implies welcoming the person regardless of everything.

'The wonderful thing about the grace of God is that it is like the Spirit herself: it is no respecter of persons or of theological boundaries. Although I, as a Catholic, value the sacrament of reconciliation and find it a powerful invisible sign of God's invisible grace, I do not for one moment think that God's grace can be confined. The grace of God is like our child's conception of a raygun – it is invisible, all penetrating, defies all barriers.

'I've no idea if this is orthodox theology, nor do I particularly care, for I speak of what I see, of what I experience day by day. I have learned long since that Christians have no monopoly on goodness, that unbelievers are as capable of heroic generosity as anyone. In short, that the Spirit listeth where it will.'

During her years among the dying, many of Sheila's Catholic concepts have fallen away. 'I have a lot of church friends – Anglican ministers, Catholic priests, monks, Jesuits – and I suppose I cling to the Church with my bleeding fingernails because these people remain within it. I don't feel a vast need to belong but I do feel a need for friends and fellow searchers. I go to Mass on Sundays, because the Eucharist and the mystery of the Liturgy are important to me and I have the roots of obligation that all Catholics have. And usually I'm glad I've gone.'

After twelve years at the hospice, Sheila has now moved on to new work as an expert in pain control in a large hospital. She is advising doctors on the treatment of the dying and is particularly concerned with children who have cancer. She now feels herself to be fulfilling the gifts that God gave her and also to have become even closer to God.

'There are two levels. There's a very deep level of closeness to God which is one of unbelievable joy and yet that level is absurdly compatible with being angry or depressed. It's like the sea – down at a deep level my life is very still whereas on the top there are all sorts of storms.

'When I'm very distracted I tend to pray more in words – when I'm still I pray without words. But when I'm distracted I do talk to God in a way which a few years ago I would have despised, because I like to think of myself as a serious, contemplative person and now I don't think it actually matters a bit.

'Sometimes I think the very childish relationship I have with God at the moment is quite peculiar and other times I think it completely natural. I feel that I live in the presence of God all the time. It's like a compass and needle – the moment I'm alone, I'm liable to flick back, to consciously avert to God. I don't spend as much time in formal meditation as perhaps I should. Probably half an hour a day come rain or shine and five hours a day on retreat, which I do every three months or so.

'I see going on retreat as going into the desert and I think someone as active as I am needs to go into the desert to centre down and to really listen and to say, here I am, I've come to do your work, speak to your servant. And then to listen – and to go with no books, absolutely nothing, so that you can really expose yourself to God. It can be quite a stormy time although it's been unstormy for me in the last few years.

'Giving myself completely to God in the midst of torture was the most fundamental experience of God in my life. I think that was a real watershed and the key to my spirituality now is cleaving to the will of God. So the reason I go on retreat is not so much to experience God because I think there's a sense in which that doesn't actually matter. It's a gift, but I think one should be indifferent to one's sense of the presence of God. I go in order to listen, it's my way of obedience. So if anything matters to me, it matters to do the will of God.'

But although Sheila's experiences of God are so clear and her nature, being a flowing one, is always flowing in that direction, yet she has been forced to doubt very deeply.

'Over the last few years, so many bits have dropped off my image of God that I have sometimes thought I was going to lose my faith altogether. This shedding has been a continuous process but there was a time of crisis when a particularly large piece of my God concept fell off. It was a psychologist who dislodged the fragment although I suspect it was already loose. It was because the more I learned about psychological functioning the more I realized that there is a rational scientific explanation for many experiences which people call religious.

'What shook me most was when I was forced to question my own twenty-year experience of being pursued by God. I had for many years identified with the poet Francis Thompson in his 'Hound of Heaven'. I had thought of myself as hounded by God, called to his exclusive service in a way that marked me out from my fellows. Painful as this had always been, I found it infinitely *more* painful to face the fact that perhaps my sense of calling was more a product of childhood conditioning than the intervention of God. It's difficult to explain just how rude was this awakening. At forty-eight I had to open myself to the possibility that the fundamental premises on which I had built my life were false. If I wasn't a woman called by God, who was I? A pious deluded fool? A religious nut? Painfully I struggled with these questions till they brought me face to face with what is for all of us the ultimate question. Is there a God at all? For several months I lived in a sort of void. I knew what it meant to be an agnostic. To simply *not know* if there is a God or not.

'This doubting was not just an intellectual and emotional experience, it had considerable practical consequences. As a serious believer my life is, to a large extent, geared to the worship of God. I pray regularly every day, go to weekly Mass, I give religious lectures. What then was I to do with my newfound doubts? Should I cancel a retreat I was scheduled to give in the States? Go public and declare that I no longer believed what I had been preaching? Or should I go on as if nothing had happened, keep on with all the comforting God talk, and rot my soul with hypocrisy?

'In fact I did none of these things. I confided my anguish to a few of my closest friends. They counselled me to stay with the question, to live in total honesty and openness to the unknowing, however painful that might be. One friend told me: your questions are not to be answered but to be lived with.

'So I waited, like a sailor becalmed or a hill walker overtaken by mist. I had no idea how long it would be or, indeed, if the mist would ever lift. I continued to pray in so far as I was able. I kept on going to Mass, though it left me cold. And then, one day, sitting by a swimming pool in Florida, I found that the mist had lifted. The passages in the Bible that I was reading in preparation for the retreat that I was to give, began to speak to me again. The dead letters came alive once more, the dry bones became clothed in flesh and began to dance.

'I've reflected a good deal of late on this experience of unbelief. Inevitably, I ask myself, why? Had I become, without knowing it, unfaithful? Am I becoming too enmeshed in a materialist society? Or was it perhaps a time of testing, of spiritual growth? I have no clear answer to these questions, perhaps there's an element of truth in each of them. What I learned however or, rather, rediscovered, is that faith is a gift. It is not an intellectual process. It's a movement of the heart towards things unseen, unheard. Like Moses, we hear a voice behind the tree, thunder in the mountain top, and we're done for. Life is never the same again. We are branded, left drooling, thirsting for something or someone we've never seen.

'Since then, I've learned to pray because God is. Because the very existence of God draws out of me this need to pray. And because prayer is a way of letting God blast his way into our lives and transform them.'

Bibliographical References

SHEILA CASSIDY
Sharing the Darkness, Darton, Longman & Todd, 1988.
Good Friday People, Darton, Longman & Todd, 1991.
Audacity to Believe, Darton, Longman & Todd, 1992.
Light from the Dark Valley, Darton, Longman & Todd, 1994.

JUNG CHANG
The Wild Swans, HarperCollins, 1991.

VIVIANNE CROWLEY
Wicca, The Aquarian Press, 1989.
Phoenix from the Flame, The Aquarian Press, 1994.

ANNIE DILLARD
Pilgrim at Tinker Creek, Pan Books, 1976.
Holy the Firm, Harper & Row, 1977.
Living by Fiction, Harper & Row, 1982.
Teaching a Stone to Talk, Harper & Row, 1982.
Tickets for a Prayer Wheel, Harper Colophon, 1986.

SUSAN HOWATCH
Glittering Images, HarperCollins, 1987.
Glamorous Powers, HarperCollins, 1988.
Ultimate Prizes, HarperCollins, 1989.
Scandalous Risks, HarperCollins, 1991.
Mystical Paths, HarperCollins, 1992.
Absolute Truths, HarperCollins, 1994.

ELAINE MACINNES
Teaching Zen to Christians, Theosophical Publishing House, Manila.
Obtainable from Prison Phoenix Trust, 4 Osborne Close,
Upper Wolvercote, Oxford OX2 8BQ.

IRIS MURDOCH

The Nice and the Good, Chatto & Windus, 1968.
The Sovereignty of the Good, Chatto & Windus, 1970.
The Sea, The Sea, Chatto & Windus, 1980.
The Philosopher's Pupil, Chatto & Windus, 1983.
Acastos, Chatto & Windus, 1986.
Metaphysics as a Guide to Morals, Chatto & Windus, 1992.
The Green Knight, Chatto & Windus, 1993.

MA YOGA SHAKTI

Chandogya Upanishad, Wilco Publishing House, Bombay, 1976.
Yoga Syzygy, Ma Yoga Shakti International Mission, 1984.
Hanuman Chalisa, Ma Yoga Shakti International Mission, 1986.
A Spiritual Message, Yoga Shakti Mission, 1991.
These books can be obtained from Yoga Shakti Mission,
3895 Hield Road N.W., Palm Bay, Florida 32907, USA.

MARIANNE WILLIAMSON

A Return to Love, HarperCollins, 1992.
A Woman's Worth, Random House, 1993.

DANAH ZOHAR

Through the Time Barrier, William Heinemann, 1982.
The Quantum Self, Bloomsbury, 1990.
The Quantum Society, Bloomsbury, 1993.